the art of happiness

FULFILMENT AND THE HUMAN MIND

JOAN WHITE

TURNSTONE PRESS

Published by Turnstone Press
Author contact: joanwhitewriter@gmail.com

A catalogue record for this book is available from the National Library of New Zealand.

ISBN 978-0-473-74944-6 (paperback)
ISBN 978-0-473-74945-3 (EPUB)

contents

This book is dedicated to all who walk in sadness. May its words be a light upon the happy path so you may find happiness and walk always in its way.

introduction

WHY I WROTE THIS BOOK
AND WHAT IT'S ABOUT

This book is about being happy even though our lives are hard. Modern life is difficult, let's not pretend. As modern humans, we are out of our comfort zone. To survive, both physically and emotionally, we have to do many things that don't come naturally, and we have to not do, many things that do come naturally! It is as if we were swimming camels.

It's common to find ourselves treading water, not making progress towards our goals, barely holding our heads up in a flood of problems. And we all know people who have gone under, sinking into the waters of despair. Some come back up, but sadly many of us have personal knowledge of fatal events where someone we knew and loved, did not come up again. Maybe they would still be swimming beside us if they had been wearing some water wings.

Camels can swim, and when they have to, they do (there are some fascinating videos on YouTube), but camels aren't well adapted for swimming. Except for India's salt marsh camels, swimming isn't part of a camel's usual behaviour. Camels are adapted to life in dry sandy places. When they are in the water, they are out of their comfort zone. Swimming camels could use some help. They could use water wings, and, frankly, so could humans living in the 21st century.

Human minds and bodies evolved to suit tribal life in savannahs and forests. We are adapted to live active lives, eat natural foods, and experience close relationships with those around us. For nearly everyone today, no matter where they live on the planet, that is not what they are experiencing!

Our biology and our psychology don't suit modern life, or more to the point, modern life with its rush, social isolation, diets dominated by ultra-processed food, lack of exercise, etc., doesn't suit us! This is what is called an evolutionary mismatch.

If you are suffering emotional distress, do not blame yourself for being a camel, designed for desert living, for trying to walk in a flood, and finding it isn't working. We are none of us cut out for this.

Evolutionary mismatch underlies the current epidemic of chronic physical illness, things like obesity, diabetes, hypertension and so on, and also the current epidemic levels of human emotional and psychological distress. All these, therefore, can be seen as fundamentally societal problems. There are people, and groups of people, working tirelessly to

try to align human social structures and living environments with human needs. This is extremely important and
valuable work, but seeking to change human living conditions is not what this book is about. The focus of this book is
how to do okay in the here and now, how to swim and not to
drown.

While mental and physical health are closely linked, this
particular book is limited to discussing ways to overcome the
adverse effects that modern living conditions have on our
emotional and psychological lives.

I am firmly convinced that pharmaceuticals, in all but the
most severe and short-term situations, are not the best
approach to psychological and emotional distress. I wrote
this book of thoughts to talk about things that have helped
me, helped those I love and helped individuals I have
supported.

This book borrows much from Acceptance and Commitment
Therapy (ACT). ACT is a member of the family of psychological therapies that developed under the big umbrella of
Cognitive Behavioural Therapy (CBT). ACT differs from
traditional CBT in several ways, including ACT's greater
focus on accepting emotional experiences. ACT was developed in the 1980s, above all through the work of psychologist Steven C. Hayes, a professor at the University of Nevada.
For an ultra-brief explanation: ACT holds its methods within
its name: **A**ccept thought and emotion, **C**hoose values and
Take action. For interested readers, an in-depth account of
ACT and its methods can be found in *Acceptance and Commit-*

ment Therapy. An Experiential Approach to Behavior Change
(Hayes et al. 1999).

Over time I have increasingly seen that ACT draws on an
enormously deep and broad heritage of human wisdom, and
that much that is useful, but would not have gained easy
acceptance within secular and academic psychology, was
omitted. In light of this observation, my views and
approaches to helping myself and others have broadened.
While this book owes much to my training in ACT, it is not
an ACT book.

Some source material for this book started life as diary notes,
some started as emails to people who were experiencing
emotional and psychological distress whom I was support-
ing, some started as notes for friends or family members and
some sections started as personal spiritual reflections.
Because of this, certain elements are covered more than once
from a slightly different point of view with a slightly
different emphasis. I hope you will find these repetitions
reinforcing.

IT MATTERS HOW YOU FEEL AND HOW YOU LIVE

I am glad you are reading this book. I am glad because it
means you care about being happy, and you want to extend
a hand of assistance and support to yourself. You picked up
a book that claims to be about how to be happy, how to
stay afloat in a flood of problems and started to read it. It
means that however stressed, unhappy, lonely or afraid you

are today, you already hold the keys to happiness in your hand.

It's not that this book holds the keys. The keys are things you already have, that you have proven you have by starting to read a self-help book. This book is about how to find those keys within yourself and how to use them, so you can unlock the barriers between you and a life worth living. This is important, so I will say it again, choosing to read this book proves you hold the keys. So what are these keys?

The first is a key of compassion, a key of care, a key of *love*, both love for others and love for yourself. Life's pain and disappointment has not destroyed that love within you. You care how you feel, and you probably care about a whole lot more besides. This is love enough, it's enough to guide you, enough to grow. You can use the key of love to test barriers and locked doors. It will tell you which barriers you should break down and which should remain. It will tell you which doors you should unlock and which should remain locked. It will give you direction in life.

Hope is a second key. Just as it did with love, picking up a self-help book proves hope is alive in you. You have hope for change, for things to get better. Hope will keep you going. Hold it tight. Don't give up. Two keys so far: love and hope.

Shall we find another key? St. Paul in a letter he wrote to members of the early church in Corinth (1 Corinthians 13:13) said three things continue forever, love, hope and faith. We have already found love and hope; is it possible we will find faith too? Faith can be the hardest of these three keys for a person of modern times to find. Not because it's not there, but because we don't call what we have by that name.

Imagine being asked if you have any *nightshade*. If you think only of *deadly* nightshade, you will likely say, no. But if you think a bit more broadly, you might say, yes, because potatoes, tomatoes and capsicums are all plants of the nightshade family. So it is with faith. To find it we don't need to go off looking for something unusual, something we haven't got, and maybe haven't seen. We only need to look for something common, something easy to find. Faith in the sense I use the word, means believing you and your choices, however small, matter, that what you do and say has consequences, consequences that ripple out across time and space, and make a difference. These expanding and enduring consequences were described by the American poet Henry Wadsworth Longfellow as 'footprints in the sands of time' in his poem "A Psalm of Life" first published in 1838 from which the following extract is taken:

> *Be a hero in the strife!*
> *Trust no Future, howe'er pleasant!*
> *Let the dead Past bury its dead!*
> *Act,— act in the living Present!*
> *Heart within, and God o'erhead!*
> *Lives of great men all remind us*
> *We can make our lives sublime,*
> *And, departing, leave behind us*
> *Footprints on the sands of time;*

Footprints, that perhaps another,
Sailing o'er life's solemn main,
A forlorn and shipwrecked brother,
Seeing, shall take heart again.

Viktor Frankl, Austrian psychiatrist and Holocaust survivor, said in his iconic memoir *Man's Search for Meaning*:

Death is a meaningful part of life, just like human suffering. Both do not rob the existence of human beings of meaning but make it meaningful in the first place. Thus, it is precisely the uniqueness of our existence in the world, the irretrievability of our lifetime, the irrevocability of everything with which we fill it – or leave unfulfilled – that gives our existence significance. But it is not only the uniqueness of an individual life as a whole that gives it importance, it is also the uniqueness of every day, every hour, every moment that represents something that loads our existence with the weight of a terrible and yet so beautiful responsibility! Any hour whose demands we do not fulfill, or fulfill half-heartedly, this hour is forfeited, forfeited "for all eternity." Conversely, what we achieve by seizing the moment is, once and for all, rescued into reality, into a reality in which it is only apparently "canceled out" by becoming the past. In truth, it has actually been preserved, in the sense of being kept safe. Having been is in this sense perhaps even the safest form of being. The "being," the reality that we have rescued into the past in this way, can no longer be harmed by transitoriness.

Doctor, missionary and musician Albert Schweitzer (1875-1965) said:

> No ray of sunlight is ever lost, but the green it wakes into existence needs time to sprout, and it is not always granted to the sower to live to see the harvest. All work that is worth anything is done in faith.

More recently, New Zealand composer Colin Gibson wrote *Nothing is Lost on the Breath of God,* a beautiful hymn based on the following scriptures: Psalm 23, Psalm 116, Isaiah 43:1-7 and John 11:1-45. The hymn includes the following words:

> *God's heart is love,*
> *and that love will remain,*
> *holding the world forever.*
> *No impulse of love,*
> *no office of care,*
> *no moment of life in its fullness;*
> *no beginning too late,*
> *no ending too soon,*
> *but is gathered and known in its goodness.*

All these writers are expressing their faith that what they do and what other people do matters. Believe it for yourself.

Flames of love, hope and faith are alight within you. I know they are there. If you are still not sure, no matter, let us start on a journey together and maybe as we go, they will burn brighter. Love will shine from you onto others. Hope for yourself will mean you can hold hope for others. Believing *you matter* means believing *everyone matters* and when you help others they know that they do.

ONE

it's all about you

WHAT IT IS TO BE A HUMAN PERSON

You are special. You are part of humanity. *Humanity*, what an extraordinary word! It has multiple related meanings. Firstly, it means being human. Secondly, it means human beings collectively, that is, together we humans are humanity. Thirdly, it refers to those fields of learning that focus on what is unique about ourselves as a species: art, music, literature, religion, philosophy and so on. That is to say, it refers to those things humans have but other animals don't have, and these are the things studied in the humanities departments of universities. Last, but not least, in fact to my mind, more important than any of the three previous definitions, humanity is a virtue. Humanity is what makes a person *good*. Here is a Wikipedia's definition of this fourth meaning of humanity:

Humanity is a virtue linked with basic ethics of altruism derived from the human condition. It also symbolises human love and compassion towards each other. Humanity differs from mere justice in that there is a level of altruism towards individuals included in humanity more so than the fairness found in justice.

Humanity is the idea that trees as well as forests matter, that the world is to be saved not by grand utopian movements but by individual acts of love. We are to treat each other as ends and not as means. This concept of care for individual people was central to the teachings of Jesus, seen in his parables "The Lost Sheep", "The Lost Coin" and "The Prodigal Son".

What is a thing? A thing is an object without agency, without will or power to act. A thing doesn't get to control its actions. It doesn't make choices. It has no capacity for knowing right from wrong. A thing has no responsibility because it has no autonomy. It has no choice, and so, it is always innocent. A spoon is a thing, so is a sword.

We, in contrast, are not things. We are not things to be used, to be abused, or to be made means to any end, by any person. We are not to be disposed of, nor to dispose of others. We are not to be disregarded, nor to disregard others. We are not to be denied choice, nor to deny choices and autonomy from others. We are not to be denied speech and freedom, nor to deny them to others. If we do wrong, if we cause harm, we are not innocent, for we are not tools, we are not wielded by another. Our actions are our own.

These rules of humanity apply to everyone, every one of the billions of us. We are to be a *kingdom of ends* as described by Enlightenment thinker Immanuel Kant.

Of all the living things on our beautiful world, you belong to the species with the greatest capacity for reason. You understand the differences between right and wrong, between kindness and unkindness and between justice and injustice. Because you understand these distinctions, and have the freedom to choose to do, or not do, any action, you have moral agency. With that freedom, with that agency, comes the responsibility to act with wisdom and with kindness.

Notice, we have in English (and quite possibly in other languages too) the same word for people, that is humanity, as we have for kindness. Don't you find that interesting? I do. *Kindness* is how we have decided to name our collective selves. And we call ourselves *wise* too. *Homo sapiens,* our species name, when translated from Latin means wise *(sapiens)* man *(homo)*. Can we as individuals of that species prove it is more than a name? Can we live up to our name by showing humanity and by being wise? We will if we try, each of us, to be the best person we can be.

THE MIND IS NOT ONE

I believe all parts of you (and of me) are good. All parts have a role and a purpose. That includes the parts of your brain that have their counterparts in the brains of other animals.

In the 1960s Paul MacLean, an American physician and neuroscientist, developed a model of the way our minds work based on the idea of evolutionary brain layers (MacLean, 1990). The model is called the triune brain concept. Because it is a model, it shouldn't be taken literally as a guide to the actual anatomy and function of brains, but it is a good starting point in attempting to understand ourselves psychologically, both what we share with other animals and what makes us unique.

The model asks us to think of ourselves as having three separate minds which work together as a team to help us live safely and well. Each mind corresponds, in a very general and simplified way, with one of the three evolutionary layers of our physical brain. According to the model, our brain evolved in stages. In the centre is the oldest layer called the reptilian brain or amygdala. The next layer is the mammalian brain or limbic system, and on the outside is the neocortex or new brain.

Because the more recent layers were added without any real updating of how the older parts worked, over time our brains have become like a large rambling country house. Imagine that this house started as a cottage and had extensions over the years without any remodelling of prior work. First, there was a ground floor extension and then later a second storey was added. In other words, newer and more complex layers have been added around and over the top of more primitive brain layers during our evolutionary journey. The cottage or reptilian brain is still there in the centre of a human brain, and so is the limbic system or ground floor extension, with the neocortex like the second storey on top of it all. Therefore, we humans share much with other animals, and with our fellow mammals a great deal.

The innermost and oldest part of the brain is responsible for keeping us alive. It regulates breathing, heartbeat and all the automatic life-sustaining functions of the body. It feels fear, hunger, anger and other basic and very essential emotions that help an animal survive in a dangerous world. But it is not capable of conscious thought or language. It acts on instinct. Its agenda is survival. Its reactions are lightning-fast, like a lizard darting into a hole.

On top of, and around, the reptilian brain, is a middle brain layer called the limbic system, sometimes referred to as the mammalian brain. It is also responsible for generating emotions, but instead of those basic ones that reptiles feel: hunger, anger, fear, sex drive, etc., the mammalian brain is responsible for more complex emotions like the sense of belonging, loyalty to one's group or clan, jealousy, prejudice and affection for offspring. The mammalian brain's emotions facilitate group behaviour and much else besides. Both the amygdala and limbic system are capable of learning, remembering and adapting. Together the reptilian and mammalian brains form the emotional mind.

The third layer, called the neocortex or new brain, is the most complex. This layer began development with lower mammals and is most developed in humans. It is the home of higher reasoning, symbolic language, imagination and creativity.

Something important to understand and remember when thinking about human emotional responses is that the difference between the emotional reactions of a small child or animal, and those of a mature reasoning human is not due to change in the amygdala nor it is due to change in the mammalian brain. It is due to the strengthening of the observing mind, which like reason, logic, language, creativity, etc., is a function of the neocortex. This brain function develops in the neocortex as we grow up and allows us to make conscious and voluntary decisions about the things we choose to do, or not to do. The observing mind is like an internal team leader responsible for what is called executive function. In the next few sections, we will continue our discussion of the layers of the human brain.

THE INNER ANIMAL OR YOUR EMOTIONAL MIND

Our emotional brain has as its job providing a burst of pleasure to make us feel good (for a little while at least) or administering a little burst of emotional pain to make us feel bad. It does these things to encourage us to act in ways that our emotional mind "thinks" will improve our chances of survival and/or our chance of passing on our genes, and to discourage behaviours and situations that the emotional mind "thinks" might kill us or reduce the chance we will pass on our genes to future generations.

As a general principle, the responses of our emotional brain are those likely to be beneficial to an animal surviving in the

wild. The older inner layer of the emotional mind is responsible for basic lifesaving emotions. The next layer is responsible for more complex emotions. Actions and events, that in
our evolutionary past, were linked to an increased chance of
survival, feel pleasurable, while those linked to an increased
risk of death feel unpleasant. For example, we are afraid of
things the emotional mind believes could harm us. This fear
may be instinctive, like the fear that causes a goldfish to dart
under a waterlily leaf when a shadow appears above it, or
learnt by association with experienced pain.

In the case of basic emotions like tiredness and hunger, it's
easy to see the connection between the emotion and a
behaviour that is good for us. We feel tired because we need
to sleep. We feel hungry because we need to eat. The
reptilian brain makes it feel bad to be hungry and good to
eat, bad to be too hot, or too cold, and good to be the right
temperature. Our reptilian brain makes obtaining good
things feel good, which is the reason why *retail therapy* may
feel pleasant until we realise how much we have spent.

Creating fear, felt as the *fight or flight* response, is the job of
the reptilian brain. Fear helps us get away from danger, or be
prepared to face it if we must. When we are afraid, blood is
diverted from digestion to our leg muscles, getting us ready
to run. Our pupils dilate. Our sense of pain is reduced and
our hearts beat faster and harder. If your reptilian brain
"thinks" fighting is a better option than running, then it may
generate more anger than fear. Frequently it isn't sure
whether fear or anger will serve you best and so it decides to
create both at once. Whether we feel anger, fear, or both

together, much the same bodily changes occur: fast heart, increased blood pressure, less sensitivity to pain, etc., because bodily responses to anger, like those to fear, are mediated by the hormone adrenalin. The message the reptilian brain sends out is, "Red alert! Battle stations!" And so, our adrenals "act now" releasing a surge of adrenalin before we even have time to assess a situation. The point is, we are quick to feel anger and fear. We feel them before we have time for rational thought.

Rational and considered responses take time, and that is why we should not act immediately in response to anger, fear or other strong emotion. Instead, keep control of your body so you have a chance to think before taking action. Slow down, count to ten, give your neocortex time to assess the situation. Remember, as humans, we do not have to agree with the suggestions about how we should act that our emotional brains make. Our neocortical executive control function can and should have the final word.

The reptilian brain reacts to *both* what the senses tell it is happening in the real world, *and* to what is happening in the verbal and imaginative mind when it decides what emotional state to respond with. That is, it gets messages from the ears, eyes, skin, nose, internal organs, muscles, etc., throughout the body about the body itself: its temperature, position, movement, etc., what is in the environment right now, *and* messages about what's playing on the movie screen of thought. The amygdala or reptilian brain has a very hard time understanding the difference between inputs from the senses (reality) and inputs from thought and imagination (fantasy). We'll be covering in more detail how the inability of the reptilian brain to distinguish real from unreal relates to human emotional suffering. (See 'Loneliness as an example of how human emotions go awry' in Chapter 3.)

The inner brain layer also has the job of directing reflex body movements, again aimed to prevent injury or death, for example, making you drop a hot pot or put your hands out when you fall, or close your eyes when something comes towards or touches your eyes. These sorts of things bypass the slow neocortex or new brain completely, and in doing so are often lifesaving or injury-preventing. Your reptilian brain has probably saved your life many times already. Survival, survival, survival – that's the reptilian brain's imperative.

The complex emotions generated by our mammalian brains are also systems of emotional reward and punishment designed to motivate or discourage behaviour, though the links between feelings and actions may be a little less obvious at first. The mammalian brain or limbic system is more complex and more subtle than the reptilian brain, but it's still ancient. It is capable of more complex feelings and behaviours than the basic *life or death now* ones, which are the responsibility of the amygdala. Think of the mammalian brain as your inner wolf or sheep, as compared to the inner reptile we have already been discussing. The mammalian brain, like the reptilian brain, is an unreasoning thing. Have you tried reasoning with your pet cat or dog? It is without language and completely without our human sense of right and wrong. Without a sense of right and wrong, the mammalian brain is, like the inner reptile, innocent of any evil. It is to be cared for and guided, not to be judged. It doesn't choose the way it feels. It simply feels the way it does.

In case you are starting to feel uncomfortable with the idea you have a wolf or sheep in there as well as a lizard, remember these are all *metaphors*, just ways to think about complex things by reference to other things that are easier to understand. There are no animals in there. The triune brain model itself is just a model, or metaphor, to aid understanding, but it is true that parts of your brain function and feel very much as animal brains do.

Like the reptilian brain, the mammalian brain receives inputs both from our senses about the real world and from the imaginative neocortex about what you are thinking. The mammalian brain is a little better at differentiating the two input sources, a bit more capable of knowing the difference between real and unreal than the reptilian brain. We don't usually feel quite as proud of ourselves just imagining achievements, as when we do when we actually achieve them. Imaginary friends are usually not quite as satisfying as real ones, etc. To a limited extent, the limbic system or mammalian brain knows thoughts aren't real, although under the influence of a truly great imagination its limited reality check function is prone to failure.

So back to the emotions of the mammalian brain. These emotions motivate complex behaviours that we share with our fellow mammals. In other words, the emotions of the mammalian brain improved the survival chances of our wild mammalian ancestors by promoting social behaviours associated with success in staying alive and having offspring.

The limbic system is thus an important part of us, capable of many multifaceted responses and feelings. Like the emotions of the amygdala, some of these emotions feel pleasant, and some, as we all know, do not. Whether they are pleasant or unpleasant, they are designed to motivate us to do things that in general are good for wild mammals by providing an emotional reward i.e., pleasure; and not to do things that aren't, or at least not do them more than once by providing a punishment, i.e., emotional pain.

Loneliness motivates social connection. Parental love motivates caring for infants and therefore enhances the success of reproduction in mammals. Envy, the *keep up with the Jones* emotion, makes us want to obtain things which have been obtained by others, things which the limbic system in its limited understanding of the world, thinks would be good for us to have too. The sense of possession or ownership is designed to help us keep hold of the good things we already have. The limbic system generates jealousy when others threaten or seem to threaten to take them away from us. It generates shame, regret, remorse and guilt, all these are subtly different emotional flavours designed to let us know that whatever we did, isn't a good idea to do again! It creates a sense of achievement or pride to encourage us to repeat or to sustain life-enhancing actions we have already taken.

It creates the feeling of belonging to, and connection with, other members of our family, clan, tribe or other special group. Being part of a group was essential to the survival of our prehistoric ancestors, and is still important today, both for our physical and for our psychological wellbeing. It is however necessary to recognise the existence of a dark flip side to our pleasant sense of belonging and the group loyalty it inspires. The flip side of belonging is the sense of otherness we feel around strangers. This feeling inspires not loyalty, but prejudice, the way we tend to treat and value people differently if they are *in* or *out* of our group. It generated the *us and them* distinction. The sense of belonging that is pleasure when we are with our friends, makes us uncomfortable in groups of unfamiliar people and shy with strangers. It makes us prefer people just like us to those who look or act differently. The limbic system creates the feeling of trust in people we know. The other side of the coin of trust we feel towards friends and family, is innate suspicion and distrust of strangers, and the painful feeling of betrayal we feel when those we trusted let us down.

Do you feel good when your nation's sports team wins a game and feel sad when they lose? Your limbic system is rewarding you, or punishing you, for your group's achievement or failure. Nothing you did. Enjoying sports and feeling good when your team wins, that's fine, enjoy it, why not? But beware and remember that this feeling is one side of an opposing pair of emotions designed to motivate group belonging. The need to belong can lead people to conform to group opinion and to take part in group actions, even when they know those actions are morally wrong.

Together the reptile and mammalian brains are sometimes called the inner child, inner animal or emotional mind. The metaphor inner *animal* does in some ways capture the function of our emotional mind more clearly than the alternative inner *child* because it isn't about being *young*. The mammalian brain or limbic system is the site of the love a human mother feels for her baby or a tigress feels for her kittens. The emotional mind doesn't grow up, it doesn't learn to reason, not ever, reasoning is not its job. Reason is the job of the neocortex. The emotional mind doesn't learn not to feel either, because feeling is its job. It can't learn not to feel any more than your heart can learn not to beat. However, the word *child* does highlight one important point: the innocence of this part of us and our responsibility to see to its needs.

It helps not at all to regard emotions as sinful or evil. Emotion is not a place where concepts like right, wrong, should or should not can exist. Therefore, it is inappropriate to judge yourself for what you do or do not feel. Your emotions are what they are, they are neither morally good nor morally bad, all of them, and that includes fear, anger, envy and all the rest. Do not judge them anymore than you would judge the feelings of an animal or young child.

It is because you are human, because you have a neocortex that can reason, that has a sense of right and wrong, that can say *yes* or *no*, to *assent* or *withhold assent* from any response, that your *actions*, but not your *feelings*, are rightly subjected to moral judgements by others and by yourself. An charging bull is not evil, nor is a cat playing with a mouse, but human actions voluntarily chosen can be morally right or morally wrong.

That is why we must take care to evaluate our emotions, both the complex ones of our mammalian brain and the more primitive ones like fear and anger generated in the reptilian brain, before we take any action. Remember that instinctive responses, even ones to real current situations, not imaginary ones, but real ones, events occurring in the here and the now, like a disagreement with a partner, work colleague, or neighbour, can be problematic or even clearly not in our own interests, however much as these emotional responses may have served our reptilian, mammal or hunter-gatherer ancestors well.

To summarize: our emotions, both simple and complex, are part of us and part of our evolutionary history. They helped our human and non-human ancestors survive in a dangerous and difficult world. They help us too, at least usually. Your emotional mind should never be dismissed as unworthy of your notice or care.

It is the source of family love and many other fine, admirable feelings. It looks to individuals and their care, it does not become overawed and driven into tyranny by visions of the "greater good" created in a neocortex that has lost its grip on kindness. It may not be capable of great humanity, but neither is it capable of gross inhumanity.

While we cannot choose to not feel what our emotional brain feels, we can keep control of our voluntary actions in our neocortex where human reason, consciousness, moral judgement and true humanity (or inhumanity) live. Listen and care, be kind, try to meet your emotional needs as long as they do not pull you away from your values. Your emotional mind cares for you, it loves you. I will say that again, it loves you, really it does. You are its number one, so care for it in return.

Remember though that a human being is called to reason, and cannot feel his or her way to a successful, meaningful and ultimately satisfying human life. This is why learning how to successfully interact with our emotional mind is one of the most important tasks of human life. Learn to listen to it and learn to care for it, but do not give over control of your voluntary actions in the world to feelings. To operate on instinct, or feeling alone, is to behave like a child or an animal. As we mature into later childhood, adolescence and adulthood, we (at least we should) develop self-control, which means the ability not to act on our emotions. Self-control is one of the several functions of our neocortex or most advanced brain layer, and as far as we know, self-control is unique to humans.

If animal metaphors don't make you feel uncomfortable, you can embrace them in your imagination, and respond to emotional suggestions you chose not to follow, with humour. How about, "Thanks lizard, but I don't need that ice cream," or "Thanks sheep, but I think I can go to the movies alone," or "Thanks wolf, but I don't need to win this argument."

We are not wolves in a wolf pack. We are not sheep in a herd. We are not even stone-age hunter-gatherers living with a small tribe of closely related individuals who need to protect and defend a territory. We do not need to struggle daily to acquire, acquire and acquire, just to get enough to eat. And so, we must be as wary of acting on complex mammalian emotions, just as we are when assessing the value of what our reptilian brain suggests we do.

You are a human being. We have already talked about how special you are. You may experience the same emotions as a sheep, but you are not a sheep forced to follow the herd without reflection. You will feel peer pressure, but you do not have to bow to it. You will fear as a lizard does, but you don't have to run in the face of that fear. You may feel instinctive distrust of strangers, you may feel the desire to establish dominance or win at games, but you don't need to be the top dog or roll over and submit to the powerful. To quote French-Swiss neuropathologist and psychotherapist Paul Dubois from his influential work *Self-control and How to Secure it* (Dubois, 1909):

> The animal thinks, loves and suffers. I know all the distance that separates the mentality of the brute from the spiritual life of man. The animal reacts more simply, obeys the impulses of his feelings, of his instincts, he lives according to nature and succeeds in that better than we do. It is only in man that we find conscience developed from what passes within him, the faculty of reacting, not on simple physiological excitations, but on

mental representations. He alone is capable of analysing, of inwardly observing, of raising himself to the abstract idea, he alone obeys moral laws which he adopts when he has learned the advantages that virtue and happiness bring.

In other words, by focussing on values we can assess what to do and get the motivation and ability to act the way we want to. Later sections will cover what values are and are not in detail.

THE NEOCORTEX – HOME OF WORDS, IMAGINATION AND REASONING

The human neocortex, which is the outermost layer of the brain, is a wonderful thing, literally a thing of *wonder*. It has many functions.

The neocortex is the home of logic and reason. With it, humans have invented computers, devised calculus, run cities, landed on the moon, and started to understand our bodies, the ecosystems of our planet and the nuclear chemistry of stars.

The neocortex is the home of artistic appreciation. With it we all can appreciate music, art and the beauty of a rainbow. And some do more, some have composed music and painted masterpieces.

It is the site of our capacity for language or our *verbal mind*. Because of our verbal mind we can understand and use words to talk to each other, to think about and describe abstract concepts and to write and read books.

The neocortex is also the site of our imagination. The human imagination is an amazing thing, powerful, terrible and awe-inspiring. With it, and because of it, humans can work for years to achieve a dream without any external reward beyond the internal ones we give ourselves. Imagination is also the source of empathy and the source of humanity. It is our species' greatest treasure but it can also be its greatest curse. There is more on this apparent paradox in 'Imagination, gift and curse' in Chapter 3.

Along with our ability to use language, to reason and to imagine, our neocortex is what gives us the ability to make moral choices. It gives us the power to do what we know is right, what will be good for ourselves or others. Sadly, but inevitably, along with the power to do good, comes the power to do evil. Power to do enormous harm, to ourselves and to others, power capable of carrying out and directing others to perform acts of inhumanity no animal could ever execute.

The neocortex gives us self-control, conscience and moral sensibility, and by giving us those things it gives us the power to do miracles. By the word *miracle,* I mean the ability to show courage without feeling it, to share with others what we want ourselves, to extend kindness beyond our own nearest and dearest, even to imagine and aspire to universal love. Acts of moral courage, conscience, and self-control. These are miracles other animals simply cannot do. We humans alone among all living things on our beautiful precious planet can choose to live by values and not by emotions. You, and other people, alone among animals, as far as we know, don't have to act the way you feel. Because of our neocortex, we can choose to love people we have never even met, support ourselves in suffering, aspire to ideals, understand the concept of the divine, and give meaning to our lives in ways animals never could.

We are a miracle.

THE CONTINUOUS YOU

Within us there is a function beyond thought, beyond words and beyond emotion. This function is called by many names, for example, the continuous you and the noticing or observing mind. This function, not the thoughts or feelings it notices, chooses what we will do with the parts of our body that are under our voluntary control, for example, our tongues, our hands, our arms and our legs. When we are centred in our noticing self, we are practising what is called *mindfulness* in modern psychology.

Along with language, imagination, creativity and reason, the noticing or observing mind is a function of the human neocortex. The observing or noticing mind does not have an exact location. It is more like something the neocortex does, than something it has. This is because the noticing mind is an *emergent property*. *Emergence* is a somewhat confusing concept. It means that when the individual parts of a complex system interact, something which is not a function of one or more of its parts, emerges. The concept of emergence is old, discussed at least as far back as Aristotle (384-322 BC).

A metaphor might help. The *noticing mind* emerges from the human neocortex as *ringing* emerges from a bell. A bell *rings*, but you can't ask *where* in a bell the *ringing* is. In the same way, the neocortex *notices*, but you can't say exactly *where* in the neocortex the *noticing mind* or *continuous you* is. Other common examples of emergence are the wheeling of a flock of birds, the behaviour of an ant colony, a tornado emerging from air, or even how the life of an individual animal or plant emerges from a collection of cells.

If the concept of emergence remains rather mysterious, that's okay, emergence does have something of the feel of spirituality or magic about it. The continuous you has many of the properties our diverse religious and philosophical traditions have attributed to *soul, conscience* or *higher consciousness*.

Let's look at what the continuous you or the observing or noticing mind does. It *continues* while thoughts and feelings and environments change. It continues as your body changes, as time passes and as you move from place to place. For as long as you live, the continuous you remains you. It is always *I*. It is always *now* and always *here*. Think of the sky. Clouds, winds, rain, sunshine, days, nights, rainbows come and go, but always the sky continues. The sky is not the weather. Stormy weather cannot damage the sky. So with the continuous you. You are the sky. You are always there. You are not the thoughts, feelings, sights, sounds, days or minutes that like weather come, and then go. Alternatively, think of a chessboard. You are the chessboard. You continue, no matter what is happening with the pieces in a chess game. So it is with the continuous you, whatever happens in the future, whatever has happened in the past, whatever thoughts, feelings or experiences you may be having right now, this part of you, the continuous you, continues.

It *notices* our thoughts and feelings (the actions of our emotional and thinking minds), whether memories, imaginings or responses to current events. It notices our environment. It notices our bodies. It controls *attention*. It decides what to pay attention to and turns the attention magnifying glass there.

It *reality checks*. It distinguishes between environmental inputs and the inputs of thought and feeling. It *evaluates* thoughts and feelings, considering them helpful or unhelpful, agreeing, or agreeing to disagree, with them and deciding how to respond to them. The continuous you has the power to give assent to, or withhold assent from, any opinion, even the opinions of your mind.

It *controls* our voluntary actions. Voluntary actions are the things we choose to do. The continuous you gives consent to, or withholds consent from, any action. It applies a moral sense as it checks potential actions for alignment with values. It is the overseer, and it has the power to give a final *yes* or *no* to any action. This aspect of the continuous you is called *executive function* and more than all its other functions it is what gives us the freedom to be the miracles we are.

A quote from Austrian 18th Century writer Marie von Ebner-Eschenbach:

> As far as your self-control goes, as far goes your freedom.

Being aware that your voluntary actions are not controlled by thoughts or feelings, but that the control instead lies in a non-verbal and non-imaginative part of your being called the noticing or continuous you, is a strange and new concept for some people. A couple of simple exercises that you can do right now, will, however, prove to you that this is true, and so I invite you to follow the instructions in the next two paragraphs before moving on.

In these exercises you will be asked to do the *opposite* of what you are thinking.

Think as hard as you can, "I will not lift my arms." Think it over and over again. Say it out loud if you are in a situation where it's okay to be talking out loud to yourself. "I will not lift my arms. I will not lift my arms. I will not lift my arms...." Keep going, get into a rhythm, and once you have a rhythm going and while you're still thinking, "I will not lift my arms," as hard as you can over and over again, *lift your arms*.

Could you lift your arms even while constantly thinking you would not? If you followed these instructions carefully, then yes you could and yes you did, because you can!

Without words and without thought, some part of you, that you are not fully aware of, can give an overriding wordless command to *lift your arms* despite anything your thinking mind may do or say.

Try it the other way:

Think as hard as you can, "I will lift my arms." Think it over and over again, say it out loud if you are in a situation where it's okay to be talking out loud to yourself. "I will lift my arms. I will lift my arms. I will lift my arms....," Keep going, get into a rhythm, and once you have and while you're still thinking, "I will lift my arms," over and over again, as hard as you can without stopping, do not lift your arms. Did you lift your arms? No, you didn't, because thoughts don't directly control your actions.

Now you know that somewhere, some part of you that you are not fully aware of can give a wordless *no* regardless of your thoughts just as it can give a wordless *yes*. You can try the same thing with, for example, I will, or I will not pat the top of my head.

Interesting, isn't it? Thoughts can't stop you doing something or make you do something. Somewhere in you, is a part of you, that while it has no words of its own, actually decides what to do, and it can do the exact opposite of what the verbal mind is saying that it wants to do. Somewhere in you, there is this deciding part called *executive function,* I suppose because that is what CEOs do. They get to decide!

being happy and being sad

TWO TYPES OF HAPPINESS, TWO TYPES OF SADNESS

Folk wisdom, by which I mean those common proverbs and aphorisms passed down the generations which offer sage advice on how to act, how to understand, and how to cope with common problems of life, teaches we have to take the good with the bad. Life is full of both pains and pleasures. There are no roses without thorns, no cherries without stones, no summers without winters. Maybe you would like to think of your own metaphor or image describing the tears and smiles, the ups and downs, the twists and turns, we all get to experience on the roller coaster of life. These natural ups and downs are associated with the first type of happiness (pleasure) and the first type of sadness (natural pain).

We feel pleasure or happiness type 1 when we experience things we like and enjoy: pleasures like a hot shower, a first kiss, a view from a mountain, the scent of a rose or the birth of a child.

The first type of sadness is the natural pain we feel when things aren't going our way. Small things, like when the car won't start, our dog vomits on the bedroom carpet, we spill our coffee, notice for the first time that our hair is falling out or going grey, or we break our favourite cup and big things too. Sooner or later something far worse than day-to-day irritations will happen: someone we love will move away or die. We might find out we have cancer or heart disease, or lose our job... It hurts; it can hurt a lot. We feel sad and that's okay, it's natural. Not to feel some unhappiness or more likely to pretend not to feel some unhappiness in such situations wouldn't be a sign of superior virtue, or moral strength, but instead be a sign of cold clinical detachment or of failure to honour the goodness of the whole of us, including our emotional core, or in fact of denying and devaluing the human heart.

Any life has its sad moments. No one can avoid them. We all experience emotional pain and physical pain. But we need not be afraid of this natural pain. We are human and have human hearts that are made to feel, to stretch, to hold together or even to fall apart at times of sadness and loss, and then come together again after the time of tears. This is what I call sadness type 1 or natural sadness.

Remember that emotional pain, like physical pain, should be regarded as a gift, for emotional pain, like physical pain, has a purpose and can help us.

Those who lose the sense of physical pain, for example, those affected by leprosy, fail to care for their bodies and slowly, by neglect, by burns, by cuts and other wounds, destroy themselves. In some cases, their bodies become so deformed by injury, that they are hardly recognisable as human. In a similar way, natural emotional pain helps us to care for our emotional selves so we are not transformed into uncaring robots who never shed a tear in sympathy or compassion. Feelings are purposeful, they are useful tools. We need to use them correctly, not throw them away. To do so is to risk becoming callous, to risk becoming an emotional leper or an emotional cripple barely recognisable as human. Never to feel sad is not a victory, it is instead a triumph of coldness.

But there is another kind of sadness much worse than sadness type 1. An unnatural type of sadness, quite different from natural sadness, one which our emotional centres were not designed to feel. This is misery which I call sadness type 2. Sadness type 2 can crush the human spirit even when circumstances are favourable, even when a person has food, shelter, company, people who care for them, all the trappings of a good life.

Reader, just now you might be experiencing this second kind of sadness: the sadness I call misery. It is a heart-breaking kind of sadness that leaves a person hurting even when the garden is full of roses, the cupboard is full of food and the sky is blue. It is the kind of sadness that walks along the beach with you, that a comedy movie won't shift for long, or maybe not at all. What I want to share with you is this: no one can avoid natural sadness, but misery is a kind of sadness that can be swept out of your life, and should it ever try to return, it can be swept out again and again. We were not made to be miserable, not made to sink into a permanent slough of directionless despair, in which moments of fleeting pleasure are like isolated sparks superimposed on a background of endless darkness.

We have touched on the first kind of happiness, which is the sense of pleasure or enjoyment which comes, stays for a while and passes away once the pleasurable circumstances that caused it end. Happiness type 2 is quite a different kind of happiness. It can be called fulfilment, contentment or inner peace and it doesn't have to come and go. The aim is to experience the natural ups and downs of human life, the times of type 1 happiness and type 1 sadness superimposed on a background of enduring happiness type 2 and not on a background of despair.

Life doesn't guarantee that happiness type 1 and happiness type 2 will always pull together. Sometimes we have to choose between them. Pleasure might suggest a lie in, but the track of fulfilment means we have to get up, vacuum the car, pay the bills and even go to the dentist. Fulfilment can be imagined as the tracks of a roller coaster taking you safely through the ups and downs of natural pain and pleasure and bringing you to the end of your ride safe. This second kind of happiness (fulfilment) goes with you even into the dark places, the places filled with pain. It went with Viktor Frankl into a World War II concentration camp, and it can go with you into, through and safely out of, whatever in life has, or may make you unhappy. It will be with you when your eyes are full of tears and when they sparkle with laughter, when the waters are stormy and when the sun shines, wherever the long and winding road of life takes you.

Happiness type 2, or human fulfilment, is like a shadow. You can't just try to grab at it, for like a shadow it is a consequence of something else and in itself it has no independent being. If we grab at the shadow, our hands will come back empty, for there is nothing there. Just as when you grab at a shadow your hand comes back empty, so will direct attempts to gain fulfilment. To gain fulfilment, a person has to aim at the thing that creates the shadow, that is, the thing that fulfilment follows.

Viktor Frankl wrote in *Man's Search for Meaning*, first published in 1946, that he found this quote helpful to people prone to despair. Despair is yet another name for that second kind of sadness I call misery which we don't need to feel.

> For success, like happiness, cannot be pursued; it must ensue, and it only does so as the unintended side effect of one's personal dedication to a cause greater than oneself or as the by-product of one's surrender to a person other than oneself. Happiness must happen, and the same holds for success: you have to let it happen by not caring about it.

So what is the thing that the shadow we call fulfilment follows? It follows living our values, committing to being our best selves in all we do. It is great when you can pursue both kinds of happiness, both pleasure and fulfilment at the same time. Find some things that make you happy both ways if you can, things like a walk, phoning a friend, etc. But don't let chasing first happiness lead you away from seeking the second. Chasing pleasure, that is happiness type 1, can become a trap when it leads us to buy into sadness that never shifts.

Paul Dubois wrote:

> What man needs is faith in an ideal of moral beauty, an attachment increasingly greater to ethical views, contributing to give him happiness upon this earth; not that happiness which is dependent on circumstances, but inner happiness entirely resulting from a complete unison between conduct and ideal aspiration...

and

> Altruism makes us think of others, of all humanity, ourselves included; we cannot seek after the good of every one without creating our own happiness. It may be mixed with troubles, but it will be the happiness of our innermost ego.

To seek a life of fulfilment in pleasure is to look in the wrong place, to search in vain, for you will not find it there.

Australian doctor and psychologist Russ Harris calls this problem *The Happiness Trap* and this is the name of his excellent, easy-to-understand and widely available ACT self-help book (Harris, 2022). I do however want to stress here that second happiness is no trap. What Russ is talking about here might more accurately be called the pleasure trap, but such a puritanical title would hardly attract potential readers the way *The Happiness Trap* does. Second happiness or fulfilment is in no way a trap, it is the path to freedom. So aim to follow Viktor Frankl and so many great human teachers, aim to do good, for that is the thing that casts the shadow that we call fulfilment.

This book is about all four emotional states.

- Happiness type 1 – pleasure or enjoyment
- Sadness type 1 – natural temporary sadness
- Sadness type 2 – misery or despair
- Happiness type 2 – fulfilment.

LONELINESS AS AN EXAMPLE OF HOW HUMAN EMOTIONS GO AWRY

There are two major ways that serious ongoing human emotional suffering is produced. The first relates directly to the inadequacy of our social structures to meet our natural human needs. The second is self-induced suffering that develops when we allow the verbal and imaginative functions of our neocortices to beat our emotional brains up. Often the two mechanisms operate hand in glove.

Painful natural emotions become a problem when flawed social structures prevent us from making the natural responses that would alleviate our distress. Let's take a closer look at loneliness. I am choosing loneliness because it is so common and so painful, and also it is a good illustration of how the two mechanisms outlined above work together like a pair of thugs.

As we discussed previously, all emotions have a purpose. So, what is loneliness for? Let's consider the case of a herding animal like a goat. Goats get lonely. If kept alone for even a few days, a goat can become greatly distressed (this should never be done). The unpleasant nature of the feeling of loneliness ensures that a wild goat stays with its herd, and doesn't wander off to become easy prey for wolves or other predators. Loneliness motivates behaviour that provides a goat with the safety of numbers against predator attack. The ability to feel loneliness promotes survival, and so in the course of evolution it has been selected for. Goats that didn't feel lonely when alone didn't prioritise coming back to the herd and so didn't live long enough to pass their immunity to loneliness onto their offspring. So it is with us. A caveman or cavewoman isolated from his or her clan or tribe didn't do very well in the neolithic survival stakes, and therefore the ability to experience loneliness was selected for in human evolution as it was in goat evolution. Loneliness is common to all herding or social animals and humans are social animals. Our natural lifestyle is the life a group, of extended family and tribe. Our experiences of loneliness encourages us to become more involved with other people, because being social and having friends and family to help us and protect us, is good for our survival. Being part of a group is fundamental to human happiness, reflecting the need our ancestors had for each other. In the natural state, as a member of a herbivore herd, or a member of a hunter-gatherer tribe, no animal or human would feel loneliness for long before returning to the fold.

Yes, loneliness is useful, normal and common in humans. It only becomes a problem when loneliness cannot be resolved because society does not offer suitable companions, or because people are cut off by disability or distance from others. Loneliness is therefore an example of the first mechanism at play in generating human emotional distress. It is fundamentally a social problem. Sadly, our modern Western democracies are experiencing a famine of connection and so loneliness is epidemic. Just as physical hunger cannot be resolved in a famine, the unnatural social conditions in which we live can result in long-term unresolved loneliness. Chronic loneliness is harmful to a person's health and that includes physical as well as emotional and psychological wellbeing.

Superficial relationships, like those so common in modern society, cannot alleviate loneliness and often worsen it. Facebook posts are a prime example, for like group conversations with casual acquaintances, typically only the pleasant is revealed into the ether. The smiling faces of advertising don't help either. People feel worse if they believe that everyone else is happy, that everyone else's life is perfect. It creates a sense of inadequacy, of failure.

It takes a deeper kind of sharing for people to learn they are not alone, that others have had similar experiences and felt similar feelings and thoughts. That other people have found a way through, and have found a way to use pain for good. It may be that reading a novel, or the book of Psalms, or watching a movie can do more to bolster our sense of connection with other people than a trip to a crowded shopping mall, or a day on social media. The increased loneliness created by many superficial relationships and the feeling that of all the people around us, no one has taken the time to know us, is perhaps why many people may feel more alone in a large city surrounded by thousands of their peers than they do when they are completely alone.

Never communicating what is really in our hearts, or hearing what is in the hearts of others, exacerbates our sense of isolation, deviation, alienation and disconnection. We only get to understand what is going on in other people's lives through closeness, through listening, through caring. Without close relationships of the kind our ancestors experienced in the tribal environment of our evolution, we are prone to start imagining that no one else ever felt like we do, or suffered like us, so no one else understands, etc. We may then develop a *woe-is-me* attitude, when what is true, is that, nothing has befallen us that has not befallen many others before. Believing mind stories about the uniqueness of our suffering multiplies suffering. And even worse, a lack of knowledge about the thoughts and feelings of others may lead us to develop the self-judging belief that we must be suffering from a mental "illness" to think and feel as we do.

We may very well add to the pain our inner selves are feeling, by telling ourselves it is our fault when we are lonely. We lower our self-esteem, beat ourselves up, tell ourselves that our loneliness is our fault, and that it is because we are not socially confident or likeable. We may tell ourselves that we better buck up, or that we are acting like a baby. What mammal, forced to be alone, would stop being lonely because it's told to stop feeling lonely? A person in a famine would eat if there was food to eat. Don't look a starving person in the face and blame them for their hunger. Letting our verbal mind go on the offensive and launch verbal arrows like these into our emotional core leads to a vicious cycle. We may even deliberately isolate further from others! If you are lonely, be kind to yourself while you try to make closer connections with others. Don't beat yourself up.

IMAGINATION, GIFT AND CURSE

Now we are getting to the heart of human emotional problems. Our thoughts, our memories and our imaginations can upset us even though they are not real in the *I, here, now* sense. And this is all because of the single input line into our most primitive emotional centre, the reptilian brain. This is the place where fear gets generated. Think about your reptilian brain, a little skink or gecko, sitting there in your head with two newer brain layers around it. How does it get the information it uses to decide what emotional state to put us in for what it thinks is our good? It has to rely on what the senses and other parts of the brain tell it is happening. It has to believe what it is told.

The reptilian brain, which has the responsibility of generating basic lifesaving emotions including fear and anger, never had to deal with two different sources of input when it evolved. Reptiles don't have imagination. Reptiles do not have a neocortical imaginative brain, and so they simply do not need two separate input lines. One is just fine. As covered in Chapter 2: It's all about you, our brains evolved in stages with the oldest layer in the centre and newer, more complex layers being added around and over the top of older layers during our evolutionary journey, without any real updating of how the older parts think and work. Like a real reptilian brain, the human amygdala has only one input system. It reacts to thoughts by creating emotions that would be entirely appropriate, entirely understandable, and even lifesaving if the events being remembered or imagined were happening right now to a reptile in the wild.

Have you ever heard of the computer programmer's saying: garbage in garbage out? It means that however good a computer is, if the inputs are faulty, so will be the outputs. It's a bit like that with your emotional responses.

The key concept to understand, one that if fully grasped can change the way you understand and relate to yourself, is that sensory perceptions of *actual reality* AND *neocortex-generated imaginative images* travel down the same brain pathways into the reptilian mind. That means that the part of us responsible for fear has no way of knowing that creations of the mind are fundamentally different from the information coming in from the senses about the real world you are in right now. It means that your emotional core doesn't understand that memories are in the past, that worries or day dreams are in the future and will probably never happen. It doesn't understand that much of the time, it's seeing a movie screen and not a view out the window. The more imaginative a person we are, the more engaged with our internal world as compared to the external world of shared reality we are, the more real those movies seem, and the more *not me, not here* and *not now* emotion gets generated.

This single line of input for both the real and the unreal explains why we get angry when we remember an injustice and why we feel afraid when we imagine unpleasant events that have not happened and might never happen! Mind's eye and real eye, they can and do generate the same emotional responses in the reptilian emotional core of us, the part that creates desire, fear and anger.

Our amygdala believes everything the imagination creates is happening right now. But that does not mean it cannot learn from past experiences, to be *even more afraid* of things it thinks are happening now. It can, it has memory. If you were burnt in the past, then thinking of fire will make you more afraid than if you had never been burnt.

The animal brain is not capable of feeling sad because others do not have things, it is entirely selfish. Our inner animals (emotional minds) should be overjoyed at the circumstances of physical plenty and comfort most of us live in. When you feel sad that others don't have things, it is because your neocortex is in *imagination* putting you, or someone you love, in their place, imagining you in those circumstances, imagining you wearing someone else's shoes. It is our neocortex taking account of the saying, "There but for the grace of God go I." Yes, that's right, I am saying here that the source of your compassion and empathy is in the images your human neocortex sends down the line to your emotional mind. Remember, a very young child does not cry that another child has no toy and a dog is not unhappy because another dog is not being played with.

The fact is, if you want to be able to love other people enough to feel with them, to cry when they are crying, to laugh when they are laughing, you have to be able to feel emotional pain in response to mind-generated images. Thus, this book does not aim to teach *detachment* from emotions, neither the ones natural to all animals, nor from those originating in the human imagination, but instead to reduce your suffering by accepting, caring for and appropriately using all parts of yourself. We can still cry or laugh alongside a friend, still allow ourselves to feel their joy or pain.

THE NEOCORTEX – FRIEND OR FOE TO OUR EMOTIONAL BRAIN

When you look at creatures without reason, by which I mean non-human animals and preverbal children, you will see that their emotional responses while informed by past experiences and memory remain appropriate to current circumstances. Animals and young children respond to what is happening to them right here and right now. A very young child does not sit crying once a toy is returned, remembering how it was previously taken from them, but he or she may well hold that toy more tightly. A dog does not fail to be happy when being played with because of imagining that the game will end, instead, they value playtime even more.

For those of us who are not living in a literal war, or amid famine, or being tortured or abused in real time, severe and ongoing unhappiness or anxiety is almost always caused by long-term arousal of anxiety and fear in our lizard brain by our thoughts. We can create hour upon hour an environment of unending stress for our emotional brain by reliving past traumas, or by imagining future pain. The situation is made even worse if we see our thoughts and feelings as unacceptable or dangerous and start to engage in an endless fight with them.

What follows is an English translation of the final verse of Robbie Burns' 1785 poem "To a Mouse" (translation/modernization/interpretation by Michael R. Burch).

> *Still, friend, you're blessed compared with me!*
> *Only present dangers make you flee:*
> *But, ouch!, behind me I can see*
> *Grim prospects drear!*
> *While forward-looking seers, we*
> *Humans guess and fear!*

The point made by Robbie is that only humans sour present happiness with thoughts of future loss and push away rays of present joy with memories of pain. The distinction between natural emotions, which are responses to the *personal here and now*, that is, what is happening to me, happening here, and happening now, and mind-generated emotions which are responses to thought is an extremely important concept.

To put it in another way: the human neocortex, which is responsible for our symbolic language, imaginative capabilities, empathy, creativity, and so much more of immense value, also creates the risk of serious emotional overload for the emotional mammalian and reptilian components of our brains. It doesn't have to be that way, but it can. The result is that humans are far more vulnerable to psychological suffering than other animals are.

A state of imperturbable emotional steadiness is not necessary for a good human life and most of us would not even desire it. We can allow our natural feelings to be what they are, choose to be a fully feeling human person and still live well guided by our values. There is no need to aim at extremes, no need to become cold, clinical or Mr Spock-like in our detachment. Star Trek fans may be interested to know that Gene Roddenberry is said to have based his characterization of the emotionless Mr Spock on his perhaps somewhat flawed understanding of Stoicism. To become emotionless would be to give up feeling value-aligned pleasures and we don't need to. We can allow ourselves to feel pleasure whenever both types of happiness align, and we can feel and cope with natural sadness, whenever it, and not pleasure aligns with happiness type 2.

Our amygdala and limbic system are quite as able to cope with what they were made to cope with, that is, help us respond to current troubles and assist us to meet current needs, as are those inside any lizard or sheep. And remember we have the added advantage of getting to decide whether to act on or not to act on its suggestions. What our emotional brain can't handle is the chronic unending abuse that we, in misunderstanding the way our brains work, frequently hurl its way. As recorded in the Gospel of Matthew, Jesus tells his followers to take one day at a time (Matthew 6:34. New Living Translation):

> So don't worry about tomorrow, for tomorrow will bring its own worries. Today's trouble is enough for today.

Jesus is not suggesting we try not to worry about today, he is not telling his listeners to stop caring about their lives and their problems. No, this teaching acknowledges human emotions allowing us to be anxious (or overjoyed) about real problems (or triumphs) today. In doing so, it accepts the natural functions of our emotional brains.

Let's be honest. Most of us are living in pretty comfortable circumstances if we take an objective look at things. We have enough food, often too much. We have shelter from wind and rain, access to emergency help in the event of fire, violent attack or sudden illness. Our ancestors would envy our living conditions.

Because the images, both words and pictures, our imagination creates in our minds feel real, imagination can either cut up our hearts and make us into broken people with tortured souls, or it can free us from emotional chains, even the natural ones that keep us acting like lizards, sheep or wolves. It is imagination that allows us to delay gratification, makes hard things doable, even makes the work of being your best self, feel good. John Milton wrote in his 17th Century epic poem "Paradise Lost":

> *The mind is its own place and in itself it can*
> *make a heaven of hell or a hell of heaven.*

What I mean is that the neocortex can create second happiness even in the presence of natural pain.

Sharing with you how to stop using your neocortex with its immense power of imagination and thought to abuse yourself emotionally, and instead learn to use its gifts to create a better and happier life for your emotional mind is what this book is all about. And more than that, this book aims to encourage you to go beyond just not hurting yourself, to instead aim at the full realisation of your humanity.

Psychologists, along with spiritual teachers of many stripes, and the sages of centuries teach people how to use their neocortex to help their inner emotional selves. All of us can learn from the collective wisdom of millennia of human existence. These teachings offer the kind of help that allows a camel to swim, or a human being to live well and be happy in a world that doesn't meet all the needs of our emotional minds. To be a whole person in a broken world, and not a broken person broken by a broken world.

We can use reason and self-control to choose to act with humanity, to live according to our values and be the best person, the best miracle, each of us can be.

We can use reason to strengthen our emotional minds so that we can be resolute in the face of risk or trauma or treachery, and bear suffering with a grace others wonder at.

As we have discussed in a previous section, the emotional brain is designed to create emotions in response to temporary external circumstances, as all external circumstances tend to be. In the ordinary course of events, when the situation that induced it passes, an emotion will pass too. Emotions are always appropriate in the ever-changing natural environments of wild creatures. They are not designed to last beyond their use-by date! A lizard sees a shadow. It feels afraid. It runs into its hole. It feels safe. A dog is thirsty. It drinks. It doesn't feel thirsty any more. A goat is separated from the herd. It feels lonely. It rejoins the herd. A mother bear loves her cubs. She cares for them. Animals can and do get emotional problems. They can and often do get depressed and exhibit signs of obsession, anxiety and enduring emotional disturbance if exposed to long-term or chronic environmental stress, such as forced aloneness, cruel treatment, closely confining captivity or constant noise. The idea that higher animals (by which I mean reptiles, birds and mammals) don't have emotions is frankly ludicrous given the fact that our emotions are generated in the parts of our brains that we share with these animals, and we see emotionally driven behaviour across multiple animal classes. Emotional problems develop in animals when an abnormal environment prevents them from making the response that would in a natural environment lead to the resolution of emotion. However, most of the time for wild animals and for little humans too, corrective responses are not prevented, and so there is no ongoing emotional discomfort. Once a stressful event is passed, the emotion soon passes. This is why animals and very young children whose imagination has not yet developed, recover well after short-term trauma.

If we use our neocortex, its imaginative and verbal abilities to feed our emotional core a never-ending diet of doom, gloom and pain, we are in effect abusing an animal. How could you expect to feel happy inside while your emotional mind, which is responsible for your emotional states, believes you are in the middle of a real-life disaster? Is it any wonder a walk on the beach isn't working to lift your gloom? You would not abuse a puppy. You would not force a donkey to carry a load that should be borne by six. Would a dog be happy even to get a bone, if you were beating it, or threatening it with a stick, at the same time? No, it would not, and neither will your emotional mind.

You can learn to use your neocortex to help rather than hurt both yourself and others. Type 2 happiness, enduring happiness, fulfilment, that is the aim, not just an end to misery: the type 2 unhappiness that probably led you to pick up this book.

So what can you do to feel happy? Be kind to yourself. Be kind to your emotional core. Start by giving it a break from radio doom and gloom (an ACT metaphor). Watch your self-talk. Watch what goes down that input line. Yes, we all talk to ourselves. Mostly we do it silently, just in our heads and don't speak out loud, but the fact is we are talking to ourselves much of the time whether others hear it or not, so it's important to notice our self-talk and how our emotions are responding to it. If you notice you are remembering unpleasant past events and feel anger or fear in response, reassure your inner self. Send some reality down that single input line into your emotional centre with words like, "That isn't real. The abuser is not here. That was over long ago. What I sent you a moment ago was only a memory and it can't hurt you. You are safe."

If the fear response has been generated in the *now* by an imagined scary future that might never happen, you could send messages like, "I appreciate all you're doing to help us keep safe, but it's ok. It was a false alarm, triggered by a thought about what might or might not happen. You can stand down," or "That was a scary thought, wasn't it? That's okay, I understand. Let's go for a walk or take a shower. I appreciate you are trying to help me. Thank you."

Turning your attention to the now (a mindfulness practice), focusing on what you can see, hear, smell and touch in the world around you, will diminish the emotional response to thought by turning your attention away from scary mind movies for a moment. It will give your emotional mind a glimpse of current reality, and along with it the chance to generate *now appropriate* emotional responses.

If you try self-reassurance and/or mindfulness, and you still feel worked up, don't be surprised or concerned if you don't feel instantly calm. It may take a while for the physiological effects caused by an emotion on your body to settle, sometimes the physical consequences of an adrenalin rush last an hour or maybe more. Your emotional mind needs a bit of time to recover from a really bad fright. Give it a little more love and reality as you would give a shaking puppy.

When you need to do something you expect will be unpleasant, or go somewhere where unpleasant feelings to *the now* may arise, say to yourself, "I know this is going to be hard, but I've got your back and we can do it." Praise your emotional self for allowing you to complete unpleasant but valued actions, for example, going to the dentist or facing a job interview. Praise yourself for taking actions that lead to long-term happiness, to fulfilment, to happiness type 2. Say to yourself, "Well done, I know that was hard for you and I am proud of you. You are so brave." The key point I am trying to express is this: we must be kind to our emotional selves. Recognise when your inner emotional brain is tired, hungry, irritable, lonely or fearful and attend to its needs. Reminding yourself of the metaphor of inner *child* is useful to moderate your demands. Don't abuse yourself for feeling anxious if you have to give a speech in public. Always be reasonable in your expectations of your emotional self.

THINK OF YOURSELF AS A FAMILY

The neocortical noticing mind functions like a team leader, or the parent in a family, and all parts of you are on the team or in the family.

A traditional metaphor in ACT practice is the driver (continuous you or noticing mind) and the passengers on the bus (other parts of your mind). This can be helpful, but imagining oneself as a *driver and passengers* may not capture the important fact that all parts of your brain and body are a team, designed to work together and with valuable roles. They aren't just a bunch of unrelated individuals on a bus. Every part of your body, every function and structure of your brain, has the same goal: your success in life. They all have the same destination, no one gets off early. All parts are part of you, and they will always travel together. All parts want you to do well and be safe. That's why some branches of psychotherapy, in particular the aptly named Internal Family Systems therapy or IFS, visualise the human situation not as a bus with a driver and passengers but as an internal family.

Because an internal family can be a really helpful and valuable way to think about yourself, it might help to discuss parenting styles briefly. Based on work done since the 1960s, parenting styles have been grouped into four main types. These are known as *authoritative, authoritarian, permissive* and *neglectful* or *uninvolved*. Consideration of these broad categories can be as useful, when we consider how we care for and guide our inner child, just as much as when we care for any actual child in our care. Are you a good self-parent, consistent, supportive, loving, guiding? Do you give yourself a break and take yourself for a walk if you need it? Being an adult means taking up the responsibility of self-parenting, it is our job now to ensure we get enough rest, enough healthy food, enough exercise, enough human company, enough playtime, etc. That is what growing up is: it is taking over the parenting role from our actual parents and learning to look after ourselves, to *self-parent*. It is up to us to see that we are praised for trying and forgiven for our mistakes. Do you forgive yourself for mistakes? Do you praise yourself for trying? Do you guide yourself to helpful actions? Do you say no to yourself when that is best for you? Do you lead yourself? Encourage yourself? Keep yourself under control? Do you prevent harm to yourself? Do you provide challenges and opportunities to learn new skills and develop a sense of the divine?

Do some research on the four parenting styles, and consider how to care for yourself in terms of these styles. If you need to move into the authoritative style, which is characterised by responsiveness, warmth and predictability, then do so.

Whether you consider your inner voices, it is not so important if you name them your precious passengers, your pet animals, your internal family, or your team members, what is important is that you listen to them all. Bullying behaviour, threats of violence, unkind criticism and unreasonable demands within the team are not tolerated. No one needs to throw a tantrum to get noticed. Allowances are made for the strengths and weaknesses of each one, so there is no need for emotional outbursts or actions controlled by fear. No one is silenced, disowned, exiled or ostracized. No voice is unacceptable, no voice is split off and labelled as *other*. The leader ensures more timid or cautious team members get a chance to speak. Everyone feels listened to; everyone feels that their contribution is valued and important.

The leader provides unity and cohesion and leads the team to function as one, achieving goals in line with values. Always, all decisions for action go through the leader, no one else gets the driver's seat, no one else gets their hands on the wheel. All team members feel safe in the care of and under the authority of the team leader, driver, self-parent or coach.

Passengers feel better when they trust their driver. They do not become alarmed if another passenger calls out in a moment of distress, "Drive over that cliff." Consider the widespread terror on the bus that such a call would cause, if the passengers did not trust the bus driver to ignore this command, or if they thought their driver might let an upset passenger take over the wheel! So as the driver, tell all your passengers that you will never drive off a cliff and never allow anyone else to either. You are the team leader. You will take care of every passenger and you will drive the bus safely home.

But, hey, let's have a laugh: with all the metaphorical internal animals we've been meeting: dog, cat, lizard, wolf, sheep, goldfish, goat, camel.... maybe for fun we could invent Internal Zoo Therapy or IZT? Why not?

IT ISN'T JUST ABOUT DOING GOOD – IT'S ABOUT FEELING GOOD TOO

We can do something about misery. There is a way to feel better, yes, *feel* better right down in the reptile and mammal parts of your brain. How? By using the uniquely *human* functions of the neocortex, imagination, language, moral sense and self-control to help rather than hurt your emotional brain.

Humans old enough to reason (from about six or seven years of age) can understand that a trip to the dentist is not a form of abuse, but one of self-care, and so can voluntarily choose to go. A non-verbal animal could never do that. We can think far ahead and plan, save money for our future, choose not to eat unhealthy foods in exchange for improved health, and face challenges with courage. We alone are capable of being brave when our amygdala is scared. Note I am talking about being scared not terrified. There is an *acute severe* response to trauma in which we humans, like other animals, may be temporarily frozen by extreme fear, and so for a short time be unable to undertake any voluntary bodily movements. This response is sometimes called, *flop and drop*. In such a state a person cannot choose to be brave and so bears no responsibility for actions not taken.

We can tell ourselves we're doing well, that a pain or problem will not last forever, and quite literally be our own best friend. In this way, we can reduce the intensity of the natural emotional distress we would otherwise feel when the present is emotionally unpleasant. Humans can therefore reduce unpleasant, but natural emotions in ways that animals cannot. We can even *feel good* about things which would naturally *feel painful* by giving ourselves emotional rewards for reaching valued goals. We humans can therefore be better off, or worse off, emotionally than our animal friends. The difference lies in our own choices, in learning to use our neocortex to help rather than hurt ourselves.

THE NEGATIVE BIAS OF THE THINKING OR VERBAL MIND

The mind keeps its eye on a threat, like a mouse watching a cat. This is why the more you worry about a thought and try to eliminate it, the larger it seems, and the more it occupies your mind. Our attention is therefore often described as the magnifying glass of the mind. Think how much more detail you can detect in anything you pay attention to. Things we think might be dangerous automatically get our attention, they go under the magnifying glass, they get more zoom-in on the screen of your mind, until sometimes they are all you can think about, they fill the entire frame and there is no room for anything else.

Thoughts cannot be removed, and while we are trying to remove them, we will be focusing on them, and they will begin to dominate our view of the world, so instead of seeing thoughts you don't like as threats and directing your attention to them, it will be more effective if you direct the magnifying glass of your attention away. Pay attention to something else, maybe the next piece of sushi on the train will be more to your taste. If you notice that you have picked an unhelpful story up, and it is now engaging your attention, you can deliberately turn the attention magnifying glass to the here and now, to the external world and the task right before you.

ACT teaches that the primary route to human psychological and emotional dysfunction is our ability to create and use language. By using words, we generate from the unreal, from memories of the past and worries about the future, from the world of imagination, a horde of frightening but fictional monsters with which to terrify our emotional core. Words are important, they are useful, but they are still words. They are names, they can create images in your brain but they cannot create reality. They are not what they say they are. They are not sticks and stones to break your bones.

Just as for the emotional mind, one of the goals (maybe the most important) of your verbal mind is keeping you alive. This is why our first thoughts and reactions to any situation are frequently negative. New things, new ideas, and new people are assessed as potentially dangerous. Both thoughts and feelings have an inherent bias to the negative when faced with change, with challenge. "Better the devil you know," and "Better safe than sorry!" are adages our brains agree with, for who wants to go, "Out of the frying pan and into the fire?"

Neither does the thinking mind (both verbal and imaginative) like to waste time. Without a task in the here and now, when it has nothing better to do, the thinking mind will dig up old problems to chew over just in case there might be something worth gnawing at still there. The more difficult or painful a past problem or situation was, the more prone to dig it up again your thinking mind will be. It does this because it thinks that *maybe* just *maybe* if it chews the problem over one more time, it might find something that could help you avoid the issue occurring again, or a different and better way to react to a similar danger.

But most times that bone is soon so well chewed over that there is nothing useful left there, every molecule of worth long ago extracted. When we find ourselves uselessly ruminating over the past, it is kinder to ourselves to keep busy and find distractions (as long as they are consistent with our values).

Our minds often come up with the most negative interpretations of current events first, and this includes its interpretations of the actions and motivations of others. Our mind's aim is safety. Safety means fast detection of any possible threat and rapid defensive action if needed. Once we understand our brain's inherent negative bias, we should work to avoid jumping to conclusions about any situation, in other words, we should never become strongly attached to the first possibility or possibilities we think of. We should not jump to conclusions, and even less should we act on our first interpretation of any situation. Stop, slow down, wait for other, and probably much more likely explanations for what has happened or been done to occur to us. When we understand that our first thoughts in any situation are negatively biased, we will look with scepticism on its first offerings, we will wait for it to offer some other ideas. This particularly applies to ascribing motives to other people's actions.

Looking at a situation we are experiencing, as if someone else and not us, were experiencing it, can help us see things more objectively. We don't see other people's thoughts so thinking from an objective point of view, can help us avoid forming or reacting to our mental illusions, be they past or future, or falsely ascribed motives and misinterpretations of other people's intentions. Objectivity thereby helps us decide what actions are reasonable, and therefore appropriate to take, in the here and now of objective reality.

The common figure of speech, "Get a grip", has a particularly interesting origin. It means to get a grip on reality, but can also be physically undertaken as a reminder to act with reason. Zeno of Citium, who was the founder of the Stoic school of philosophy in Athens in about 300 BC, advocated to his students they clench a single fist as a physical *aide-mémoire* to self-control. This physical action is a reminder of what one is trying to do, which is hold onto reality, the external here and now, and not be swept away into the *what is not*, acting on what we imagine, remember, or feel, instead of what is.

THOUGHTS ARE NOT DANGEROUS

The most important concept to avoiding and recovering from emotional problems is to learn that thoughts and the feelings they elicit are not dangerous. There is no need to be afraid of them because there is a safety gap between any idea and action. This gap is a chance to let a thought go by, without any voluntary action being taken. Voluntary actions are the things we have control over, namely the things that we choose to do and say.

The keeper of the gap which controls voluntary actions is the observing mind (see 'The mind is not one' in Chapter 2, for an explanation of this term). Your thinking mind doesn't get to make your decisions for *action*. The thinking mind is like a toddler who can yell and scream and throw a fair fit, but in the end is powerless against a parent's decision, "You are going in the car seat like it or not!" Evaluating and choosing how to respond to our emotions and thoughts is one of the functions of the observing or noticing mind.

THE MIND AS A GARDEN

Many authors have likened the human mind to a garden, but some seem to forget that no gardener is in charge of all that grows in their garden. We may sow only flowers, but weeds also grow, a fact that a look out my window into my garden proves right now. It is that way in the garden of our minds too. We are simply not responsible for the appearance of unbidden thoughts we did not choose to summon. Other people, media, entertainment, books we read, overheard conversations on commuter trains, maybe even our own instincts sow seeds too, and it is inevitable that thoughts we don't want appear. We can limit our exposure to negative influences, but to fully guard a garden in order to prevent weeds ever growing, we would have to close it off under glass. Likewise, to safeguard our minds we would need to withdraw from the world into the life of a hermit or a monk. In doing so, we would lose the opportunity to assist our fellow human beings, and even then I am not convinced it would work, not given the garden soil we would take with us. So instead understand that in a garden, while weeds are inevitable, we can choose to sow flowers too.

Many books offer thought flowers: affirmations, aphorisms, encouraging quotes and snippets of scripture, and this book too contains such flowers. Use them as you like, but please don't get so caught up in the need to control your thoughts, that you feel that the appearance of any spontaneous thing is somehow a sign of your failure as a mind gardener. That would be to deny expression to so much of yourself. That kind of garden just isn't a fun place to be! Remember that the difference between a weed and a flower is only a judgement by the gardener. It is you that gets to decide what thoughts are helpful or unhelpful, and even those found unhelpful, at least need to be heard! In choosing to admit unbidden thoughts you allow space for inspiration.

Perhaps an unbidden thought may be the most helpful one you ever had; the wind may sow a wildflower miracle. So in response to a thought, ask, is it helpful, is it kind, is it beautiful, is it in line with who you want to be or not? Will you meditate on this thought? Will you act on it? Will you water and feed it or not? Is it a flower or a weed?

We can sow thistles and weeds. We can deliberately summon up memories of pain, of trauma, of the times we felt (and by summoning the memories can feel again) that we were misunderstood, insulted or treated unfairly. We can nurse our wounds, keep them open, refuse to let bygones be bygones, and constantly inflict pain on our inner emotional selves. We can indulge in revenge fantasies or tell everyone we meet about our misfortunes, but if we want unwanted thoughts and feelings to move on, if we want a mind garden filled with flowers, we shouldn't encourage weeds.

So, if unpleasant thoughts, worries or memories pop up, notice them and ask if they are helpful. How might they be helpfully interpreted and lead to useful action? If it's not helpful simply acknowledge it. It is important to notice and acknowledge thoughts, for like a toddler, the thinking mind will get louder and louder if you ignore it. You can as some ACT therapists suggest, say, "Thank you," to your mind. Or maybe, "I hear you," or "Got that, I know.' Sometimes a firm, "Thanks, but no thanks" is the best response.

However you respond, remember that you *have* thoughts but you are not your thoughts. You don't have to agree with your thoughts. You don't have to do what they say. They don't control you so you do not need to be afraid of them.

THE DIFFERENCE BETWEEN THOUGHTS AND MEDITATIONS

The Hebrew Scriptures contain these words (Psalm 19:14. New King James Version):

> May the words of my mouth and meditation of my heart, be acceptable in thy sight, Oh Lord, my strength and my redeemer.

The psalmist is asking that his or her interests, attractions and views on what is important be acceptable to God, and guide his or her attention.

It is important not to translate *meditation* as *thought* or the meaning of this passage is lost. There is even a risk of it being harmful if it is misunderstood as suggesting God judges us on what kind of sushi the chef offers, rather than on what we choose to pick up! Unfortunately, the verse above is not the only scriptural text that can be misunderstood.

There is in the Gospel of Matthew a story frequently subjected to such an unhelpful misinterpretation. These are the words of Jesus regarding adultery in the Gospel of Matthew (Matthew 5:27-28. New King James Version):

> You have heard that it was said to those of old, 'You shall not commit adultery.' But I say to you that whoever looks at a woman to lust for her has already committed adultery with her in his heart.

Jesus is not suggesting random thoughts should be regarded as sinful. He is instead speaking of the potential sinfulness of actions deliberately taken to seek pleasure in imagining doing evil, that is, "whoever looks to lust..."

What is being said in these scriptures is not that a gardener is responsible when weeds spring up in their garden, but perhaps they have some responsibility if they deliberately sow them there, or chose to nourish weeds that randomly appear.

'THE SUSHI TRAIN'

A favourite ACT metaphor for the endless procession of thoughts our verbal minds manufacture and present to our conscious awareness is "The Sushi Train". The metaphor goes like this: we are dining in a sushi restaurant where a sushi chef (verbal mind) creates and presents sushi (thoughts) on a miniature railway for us to choose from. Because we are the customers, because we are not the chef, we don't get to decide what kind of sushi the chef makes and places on the train. But we can let unwanted sushi (unhelpful thoughts) go by and pick up only the types of sushi we want, that is, the helpful thoughts.

The mind has an endless supply of unhelpful sushi. Some favourites are, "I'm not good enough," "Why me," and "It's not fair." When your mind offers up unwanted and unhelpful sushi, remember you are not the sushi chef, your verbal mind is, and it can put whatever sushi it wants to onto the sushi train. Eventually, your thinking mind will start to see that certain flavours aren't getting picked up, and then perhaps these will be produced less often. Hard as it is to believe when faced with "I'm not good enough," "Why me," and "It's not fair," your verbal or thinking mind is trying to be helpful, attempting to give you the kind of sushi you want. If you keep picking unwanted thoughts up, your sushi chef mind will make that flavour more and more often, believing, "Hey, he/she likes shrimp and avocado, I'll make more." So we don't want to pick unhelpful stories up, instead just let them pass by. It is like walking into a store. We see many products on offer, but choose to focus on what we are interested in, on what is attractive and important to us.

Anyway that you want to picture your thinking mind, don't be afraid of thoughts and don't judge your day as good or bad based on unsummoned thoughts. Judge your day as good or bad on the voluntary actions you took. Voluntary actions can include mental actions as well as physical actions. Examples of voluntary mental actions include choosing the thoughts or feelings you focus on, give your attention to, contemplate or meditate upon. In other words, the thoughts you pick up.

FEAR AND ANXIETY

Anxiety is the special kind of fear we feel when we are under threat, but the danger is uncertain or not exactly imminent. Because anxiety is the feeling caused by imagining or anticipating danger, the experience of anxiety requires the cooperation of our neocortex. Since anxiety is at the root of the vast majority of human emotional problems, I would like to talk about it in a bit more detail. Let's start by talking about our fear response. The fear response is mediated in our bodies by the hormone adrenalin. A little bit of adrenalin helps us focus, fights drowsiness and improves concentration, it helps us to get important things done.

In more severe forms of fear when adrenalin levels are higher, we experience the classic *fight or flight* response of rapid pulse, raised blood pressure, dilated pupils, butterflies in the stomach or nausea, trembling, fast and shallow breathing, or even breath-holding, muscle tension, accompanied by the need to empty our gut and bladder. Adrenalin causes all these bodily responses. Adrenalin is a hormone released by the adrenal gland and its purpose is to get you ready to do important things, maybe to run or fight, or in the worst-case scenario, a life-threatening danger that our brain assesses we can neither fight against nor run away from, to freeze and play dead. This is what is sometimes called the *flop and drop* response. Flop and drop is an even more severe fear response than typical fight or flight. One is simply paralysed with fear.

Not all of us will experience the flop and drop response in an entire lifetime, but it is ready within us, ready to be called into action as and when needed. For anyone who has suffered a traumatic event that induced a flop and drop response, remember you were frozen, and in that state you did not have the choice to run or to fight. Whatever happened to you while you were in that state is not your fault. Do not blame yourself.

Is fear truly an unpleasant sensation? Many people enjoy it in its mild or moderate forms. They are the adrenalin junkies, the lovers of extreme roller coasters, the thrill seekers, base jumpers and hang gliders. People vary in how much they enjoy the sensation of 'thrill' but it is useful to remember that what is exciting or thrilling causes the same physiological process as the things we fear. The same fast heart rate, raised blood pressure, etc., is experienced. We may find it impossible to make the same positive judgements of our anxiety responses as we do to sensations of pleasurable excitement, but perhaps we can at least learn to view our anxiety responses as safe, if there is no real danger in the here and now. If we know that it is thought and imagination that is triggering our anxiety, things that have no actual power to harm us, then our anxiety can be safely ignored until it passes on its own. We don't feel afraid of a fire alarm if we know it was triggered by a harmless bit of burnt toast.

To explain this a bit more: anxiety is like a fire alarm, it is not like a fire. It is not in itself dangerous. Just as we should not start being afraid of fire alarms, we should not become afraid of anxiety. So when you feel the fire alarm of anxiety go off, use your neocortex, make a threat assessment. Is there real danger here and now? If not, don't make the fire alarm something to be afraid of. Don't be afraid of your physiological response to danger.

If we see anxiety as a threat, all we will get is a bigger fear response. We may set up a vicious cycle in which fear leads to more fear, until we have induced in ourselves a full-blown panic attack, which, while in no way dangerous, definitely doesn't feel good!

Anxiety snowballs, if allowed to roll and grow, can become a real impediment to progress in life. Such a condition of being anxious about anxiety, or afraid of fear, is what psychiatry calls an anxiety disorder.

This substitution process in which one becomes afraid not of something in the world, but of our emotional response to the feared thing, is the principal difference between natural or healthy emotions and unnatural mind-generated emotions. Many authors and thinkers over the centuries have distinguished between our natural, clean or healthy feelings, which we share with other animals from unnatural or dirty emotions. Dirty emotions are not generated by the events or situations we are experiencing in the real world, but by reacting to our own emotions with even more emotion. Emotional reactions to emotion are self-sustaining, they do not resolve when danger is past like the emotions of other animals do. Learning to accept temporary natural feelings of fear and anxiety and not to react to fear with more fear, is the way to avoid creating for ourselves an ongoing hell of mind-induced terror.

In many cases, we shouldn't try to avoid anxiety, for to do so is to close down one's life, charting ever-narrowing circles of avoidance, as our unwillingness to experience anxiety, closes off more and more of the world behind red danger tape. Remember that the purpose of anxiety is to protect us from danger, not to be itself feared. Knowing this, aim not to be *limited* by anxiety, as opposed to aiming not to *feel* anxiety.

So try this: if you feel some anxiety in the supermarket, don't let fear of feeling anxious lead you to avoid going shopping, for avoidance behaviour can be the beginning of agoraphobia. Instead say to your emotional brain, that you notice it is anxious, but you have assessed the situation and determined there is no fire, just burnt toast. Without the addition of anxiety about anxiety, the smoke will soon dissipate and the false alarm will pass on its own.

Shyness is a form of anxiety avoidance that results from anxiety about the thoughts and feelings of others, and it can lead a person to avoid people, especially new or unfamiliar people. Shyness is not the same as being self-contained or indifferent to the company of others. Many shy people greatly crave social contact and can make the most loyal of friends. If you are shy, let your awareness and concerns for the thoughts and feelings of others lead to empathy, and do not allow avoidance of anxiety to lead to the typical avoidance behaviour of shyness, which is constraining, and leads to loneliness and an ever-narrowing life.

In writing this book, I don't want to help you to be stronger and struggle even harder against anxiety, that isn't the answer. You are probably already trying much too hard, for the more you want to fight anxiety, the more threatening it is, and therefore the more anxious you will be. Instead say to your anxious lizard, "I understand you're worried, but it's ok. There is no real danger here."

It helps to remember that our fear response has a *gain* or sensitivity adjustment. If the gain is set too high, we become afraid more easily. Turned-up gain makes our anxiety fire alarm over-sensitive, a bit trigger-happy, so, if you feel more anxiety than you usually do, for example, when you are out and about, it may be because your inner reptile has turned the gain up.

The amygdala sets the fear response to *high* whenever we feel vulnerable, for example when we are alone, especially alone in unfamiliar territory, or when we are tired, hungry or sick. So, if you feel more anxious than you expect, maybe it means you're tired and need more rest, or that you are hungry with your blood sugar dropping. All these things make you less able to look after yourself, in response to potential conflict or danger. That is why the amygdala thinks it's a good idea to increase the sensitivity of your anxiety fire alarm. The increase in anxiety that follows is natural and normal, it's not a malfunction or a new threat. So, anytime you feel unusually anxious, do not be concerned, remember your mind is trying to help you and do not add fear of natural physiology to your troubles.

It might be you are more familiar with the increased emotional sensitivity to anger we experience when we're tired or hungry. When we are tired or hungry, we become irritable, we are easily angered, and we quickly become more angry than is reasonable. Our anger gain is set at high.

The truth is that all emotions have a 'gain' adjustment, their very own individual gain knobs. Certain circumstances, like soft music and candlelight, increase the chances of falling in love, some of feeling envy, and others of awe. The point is that there are circumstances that can increase the gain of any feeling you can name, and when the gain is set on high, it increases both the likelihood you will feel a particular emotion and the intensity of that experience when it occurs.

PSYCHOLOGICALLY GENERATED INSOMNIA

We can look at what is called psychophysiological insomnia to further illustrate the vicious cycle of a developing anxiety disorder. There is a common pattern in the chain of events that leads to the development of disabling and persistent psychophysiological insomnia. It goes like this. Something happens to worry you, maybe an exam coming up, maybe an illness in the family, maybe job insecurity and an important presentation to give at work in the morning. Thinking about it causes the release of adrenalin because your inner reptile reacts to help you cope with the stressful situation, which, of course, it thinks is right here and right now, in our bed at two, three or four in the morning, and so you have a sleepless night. When the particular stressful situation passes, the insomnia disappears. For most of us that happens over and over again during our lifetime. We have odd nights of sleeplessness during times of stress.

But what happens if you buy into the idea that it's dangerous not to sleep? If you do, then whenever you don't fall asleep immediately in a time of stress, or for any other reason, your body will release adrenalin to help you deal with this additional threat. That is, the new and extra threat of insomnia, the dangerous problem of not getting enough sleep. The more you try to fight insomnia, the more you worry about it, the more you see it as a problem, the more you do mantras, the more elaborate pre-bedtime routines you develop, the more you stay up and the earlier you get up, the more you send the message to your amygdala that the situation is dangerous. Your amygdala reacts just as if insomnia was a tiger or an enemy caveperson to run from or to fight, and so more adrenalin is released to help you do just that. What you don't want to do in such a dangerous situation is be caught napping! Soon you are on the way to developing long-term insomnia, insomnia that persists long after the event that triggered it has passed. In most cases, chronic insomnia is caused by the fear of insomnia, just another example of anxiety disorder's hallmark, fear of the fear response, fear of fear itself.

In the case of insomnia, the inflation and exaggeration of the problem is due to the faulty judgement that insomnia is dangerous and that we need to make ourselves sleep, something that we are not capable of. We can keep ourselves awake, but to fall asleep we need to step aside and let nature take care of it. At the very least if you can't sleep stay in bed and rest!

The point is that sometimes we are thwarted by working too hard, rather than by not working hard enough. So, when our emotions seem unbearable, we need to ask ourselves, "Could it be I'm telling myself I have to try harder when I am already trying too hard?"

If any of my readers would like additional help with over-coming insomnia without drugs, then I would recommend the excellent ACT-based insomnia self-help manual *The Sleep Book* by British psychologist Dr Guy Meadows (Meadows 2014).

On a lighter note, you might enjoy a few corny jokes about insomnia. It truly is better to laugh than cry!

Why did the insomniac order two loaves of uncooked bread?
He wanted to dose!
Why did the insomniac contact the Secret Service?
He wanted to be a sleeper!
Why did the insomniac lie across the railway tracks?
He wanted to be a sleeper!
Why did the insomniac go to the stables at night?
He was looking for a nightmare.
What is an insomniac's favourite song?
Any dream will do!

SADNESS

The first thing I want to say is that no one chooses to be unhappy. The idea that people are about as happy as they choose to be, is quite mistaken and unkind to those suffering from depression, and all other forms of distress. Emotional distress, including depression, is more often brought on by the exact opposite, that is, by trying too hard not to be anxious or sad and caring too much. It may be that a depressed person does indeed have the means to be happy, the keys to escape the gloom, but, he or she lacks the skills needed to find and use those keys. It's like placing a blind man in a locked room and leaving the key "in plain sight." People need to be learn how to be happy.

I do not believe that deeply unhappy people are suffering from unknown physical disease processes in the brain, but neither is their distress a conscious choice.

If we can do something concrete, something real to address the reason we are feeling sad, we should do it. If we are homesick, for example, we should at least consider going home. The kindly Doctor in Johanna Spyri's classic 1880s book *Heidi* did not suggest drugs for Heidi's homesickness, he sent her home! What happened in the years between the 1880s and the 1960s when drug treatment for emotional distress became all the rage, sleeping pills were in their heyday, and attempting to alleviate the problematic social circumstances of a distressed person all but disappeared from the practice of psychiatry? It certainly wasn't a change in human emotional needs or biology. It was instead the many changes in human society, only one of which was increased availability and clever marketing of brain altering chemicals.

Sometimes, however, the circumstances causing our sadness cannot be changed or avoided. For example, if we or someone we love is terminally ill, we have been rejected in love, or lost our job, or our home, it is natural to feel sad at least for a while since we are human. If in such circumstances we fail to accept our natural feelings, and instead indulge in unrelenting self-judgement and self-punishment, telling ourselves we should not be feeling the way we do can make a bad situation worse. Feeling sad about being sad, feeling anxious about being sad, feeling sad about being anxious, and anxious about being anxious, will set distress snowballs rolling. The inner reptile is not made to cope with chronic self-induced stress and so there is a real risk that clinical depression will result. Clinical depression means no more than a level of misery and unhappiness that interferes with a person's ability to function in society. Someone who is clinically depressed can be so sad they can't work, so sad they can't look after themselves or others. They may feel so sad that even breathing becomes a struggle. In the same way that anxiety disorders frequently develop out of the vicious cycle of being anxious about being anxious, clinical depression commonly results from being sad about being sad.

When we are depressed, our emotional brain or inner animal lives in a state of endless stress, a fantasy world of torment created by the thinking mind, by its imaginative and verbal abilities. As we discussed before, the inner emotional mind is not designed to deal with this kind of abuse, it is designed to help us respond effectively to short-term dangers, to get our current emotional needs met and no more.

The problem of adding to our sorrow was described by Paul Dubois, and in addition, the eminent doctor alluded to the help we can give to our emotional mind if we turn our neocortex to helping and not hurting:

For a long time I have told my discouraged patient and have repeated to myself, "Do not let us build a second story to our sorrow by being sorry for our sorrow." And one of my patients agreed with me, citing words of Saint Francis de Sales: "I have seen several persons who, being angry, are afterwards angry for having been angry: resembling circles made by a stone in water, for a little circle makes a larger one and that makes another." We recognise here the example of concentric circles as showing increase in our physical and moral suffering. He who knows how to suffer suffers less. He accepts the trouble such as it is, without addition to it the terrors that preoccupation and apprehensions produce. Like the animal, he reduces suffering to its simplest expression; he even goes further; he lessens the trouble by thought, he succeeds in forgetting, in no longer feeling it.

It is hard for distressed people to hear and understand the wisdom of the ages in the current times when the exact opposite is preached by the "sages" of our day, that is, the psychiatrists, and under the onslaught of drug marketing which promises complete freedom from unpleasant feelings without requiring a person to learn anything. However false those promises are, they may seem a better choice than learning to accept that being human hurts. Not all people can be convinced of the truth of words like those of Paul Dubois, Milton or Viktor Frankl. Therefore those who attempt to help the distressed should not blame themselves if not every person is receptive to their words.

I want to remind my readers that animals can and do get emotional problems. Depression, obsession and anxiety are common in animals exposed to long-term environmental stress such as aloneness, cruel treatment in captivity or ongoing noise. And animals hurt, they hurt very much under current adversity or current mistreatment. That is one disagreement I have with the ideas of Eckhardt Tolle expressed in *The Power of Now* (Tolle 1997). Tolle seems to be saying there is no pain in the *now*, and so if you only experience the now, you will have no suffering. In my experience that is far from true. Being in the now may allow only real pain to affect you, and prevent amplified pain about pain from developing, but that real present pain, be it physical or emotional, can be excruciating. So, when the now is painful, remind yourself of the impermanence of all things, "This too will pass."

But we humans can, unlike animals, become depressed in even the most pleasant of external circumstances if we use our imaginative and linguistic powers to abuse ourselves. We poke and strike at our emotional minds in the cruellest of ways, and unreasonably expect it not to whine or bite or cower like an abused dog. A dog, or a small child, or our emotional mind does not respond well to, "Buck up or I'll beat you," or "If you don't start feeling better, I will kill you." If you allow your verbal mind to constantly fire arrows at your inner emotional mind and threaten its life, for example, "I will kill myself if I don't feel better by Christmas," it will become increasingly sad and afraid.

It is not kind to who we are, to want to be something other than what we are, to hate ourselves or want to end our lives. So notice when threats are being made, notice your thoughts and promise your inner self, "I am here for you. You are safe in my hands. I will not let you be hurt whatever my thoughts are saying."

If you do not get involved in struggling with threatening or bullying thoughts, if you instead treat them as what they are, just words that cannot hurt anyone, things that have no importance, they will pass by just like unwanted sushi, clouds drifting across the sky, or leaves floating down a stream.

Here are some unpleasant types of sushi you may recognise:

1. Something bad will happen
2. Something bad happened
3. You're ugly
4. You're not good enough
5. You're a loser
6. You're a failure
7. You're stupid
8. No one likes you
9. I'm going to kill you if you stay sad
10. There's no hope for you
11. You're a sissy
12. You aren't allowed to feel that
13. You're useless
14. You're sick
15. You're broken

16. It's too late
17. There's something wrong with you
18. The world would be a better place without you in it
19. You deserved what happened
20. It was your fault
21. Things will always be bad
22. It's only going to get worse
23. Your life is ruined
24. You could have stopped it happening but you didn't
25. It's not fair!

The observing mind, the team leader, or bus driver, can, in response to any threats or insults made by the unruly verbal mind, provide self-compassion and reassurance to the emotional mind, thus reducing natural fear or sadness. If you assure your inner self, loud and clear, that even the sharpest verbal arrows are not really a threat but are merely empty words, then you will find some peace.

meditations on values

S t. Paul wrote as follows to the early church in the Macedonian city of Philippi, which was situated in the northeast of modern-day Greece (Philippians 4:8. New King James Version):

> Finally, brethren, whatever things are true, whatever things are noble, whatever things are just, whatever things are pure, whatever things are lovely, whatever things are of good report, if there is any virtue and if there is anything praiseworthy—meditate on these things.

It's not so hard to start living your values once you set your sights on being the best human you can be. Then you see that it is a privilege to help another person, to be allowed into someone's life at a time of crisis or vulnerability, because being allowed to help, means you can take another step along the path of values. Every minute and every hour spent helping others leads to our fulfilment. Good deeds make us happy. And more, according to Jesus, they are the only treasures we take with us when we die, the treasures stored in heaven (Matthew 6. 19-21. English Standard Version):

> Do not lay up for yourselves treasures on earth, where moth and rust destroy and where thieves break in and steal; but lay up for yourselves treasures in heaven, where neither moth nor rust destroys and where thieves do not break in and steal. For where your treasure is, there your heart will be also.

HUMAN EXCELLENCE

Arete is the ancient Greek word for excellence. The Greeks believed that excellence in any species was defined in terms of what made that species unique, so that, for example, an excellent dog excelled at being a dog, and an excellent horse at being a horse. Humans are separated from other animals by the ability to reason, to show self-control and to make moral choices. In other words, we can show virtue. The English word virtue has its etymology in the word *vir,* which is the Latin for *man.* Thus, the word *virtue* is closely related to *manliness,* but a better interpretation devoid of the taint of sexism is *humanity.* The virtues are *humane* ways of behaving, to exhibit these qualities is what defines *arete* or excellence in a person.

The classical virtues that Greek thinkers, like Plato and Aristotle, identified as characteristic of human excellence are courage, justice, moderation and prudence. Prudence is now more commonly called practical wisdom, street smarts or common sense. The addition of love, faith and hope added elements of Jewish moral thinking emphasised by Jesus and his followers to courage, justice, moderation and prudence and created the broader list of seven virtues to be practised by a Christian. Many more words can be added to the list of what is excellence in a human: tolerance, authenticity, constancy, honesty, patience, gratitude, humility, loyalty, cheerfulness, optimism, industry, and on, and on. Uniting all these values or virtues is kindness. Kindness, compassion or love link all the flavours of goodness, and form an overarching concept of the good, in much the same way as *sweetness* is an over-arching feature shared by all types of confectionary.

VALUES, OUR GUIDES TO CHOOSING ACTION

Everybody's lost who doesn't have a path to follow, a way to decide where to go and what to do. Values are ways of acting, ways of being. They are *good* ways to be. They are virtues. When values guide your voluntary actions, both words said, and deeds done, they move your life toward the things that matter. They move you towards being the person you want to be. Our values are questions of core identity. They are about how we define and value ourselves. They form our character. Values can always be pursued, they don't depend on circumstances. Fulfilment is found in every step you take along the path to values. We don't need to reach any particular goal to be happy when we are pursuing our values. In the pursuit of values we find that a good deed really is its own reward.

Values are not specific goals or achievements. Values are aspirational, they are never reached, never completed. They are more clearly imagined as a direction than an end. The words we choose to symbolize our vision of human perfection vary from person to person, as does the way we rank them, but there is a common core which is the humanity at the heart of what humanity dreams for itself. To get an idea of the values that mean the most to you, as an individual and unique person, think about how you would describe the actions of a person you admire, an *excellent* human you would like to emulate.

Values are very broad; each one is like an immense basket containing thousands of options for its expression, for example, there are many ways to show compassion, many ways to be kind, many ways to express creativity, thankfulness or love. The ability to express a value in action is never lost, never used up. The possibility to express a value is retained even in the most difficult of circumstances. We cannot always choose the specific means or the tools we will use to express our values, but our values can always be expressed in some small way. Even when someone is lying on their deathbed, values can be demonstrated. In a smile, a word or a squeeze of the hand, love or gratitude can be expressed. Courage can be shown.

Marcus Aurelius, Second Century Roman Emperor and Stoic, wrote in his book of personal reflections aptly entitled *Meditations*:

> I must die but must I die groaning?

Why it is that living in alignment with the deepest values of the human heart, in other words with the ideals of virtue, leads to human fulfilment, is a philosophical question that many minds from Plato on have struggled with. Some have thought it proof we carry a divine spark within us, evidence of immortality, some have argued for an entirely materialist explanation based on evolution or societal conditioning. Still others have argued that God placed in humans a desire for unity with the good, which is what God himself is, so that we will love and seek him. Many answers have been given, but for now, it may be enough to believe, what so many have observed: doing what we believe to be right is the surest path to finding happiness that humans have.

From Paul Dubois:

> Man knows how to be good as long as he gets something in return, or at least receives gratitude; he is good no longer when it becomes a question of sacrificing momentarily his own interests in order to obey an ideal of kindness. I cannot repeat often enough that this is because he is near-sighted;

he is all for the present and consequently imprudent. He does not see all the good that would result to himself and to others from a life dominated by feelings of responsibility.

American author Mark Twain famously wrote in a note to the Young People's Society of Greenpoint Presbyterian Church in 1901:

> *Always do right. This will gratify some people
> and astonish the rest.*

Set your sights on virtue and aim every moment of your life towards it. Before you take any action, consider, whether it is going to move you towards your values or away from them. You can pick your own metaphor to describe the way values guide you. Are they your guiding light or guiding star? Are they your target? Your maxim to get out of a maze? Are they your compass, your true north, your trusted guide…?

Acting in accord with values isn't always easy, but consider the importance. Some people put a lot of effort into difficult physical tasks aimed to strengthen and stretch their body, so that they can, for a short time, have the body they want to have. You need to be willing to put in the same kind of effort into following your values, strengthening and stretching yourself psychologically, so you can develop, not your body, but your *psyche,* which is of course the Greek word for *soul.*

Neil Young's 'Heart of Gold' is one of my favourite songs. I cannot be sure exactly what Neil himself meant by his lyrics, but to me, the lyrics are like a prayer, "Keep me searching for a heart of gold." In these words I find an acknowledgement of the concept of "no arrival" inherent in being guided by values. Neil does not ask to be helped to find the heart of gold, only to be kept searching. In the journey of perfecting ourselves in virtue, in coming to live fully in accord with our values, we will always fall short. "I've been in my mind it's such a fine line. Keep me searching for a heart of gold" reminds me that if we look hard enough, we will find a fine line of goodness inside, at least enough to follow, to get started on the way. Every little bit of success is the glimpse of gold that keeps one on track and keeps one's hope alive.

Goals can't be your aim when values are. It is not about achieving all your goals, not about how to become a million-aire, a property tycoon or a prince. It's not even about any particular good deed. Circumstances change and any partic-ular goal may not be reached. So be proud of moving towards your values but don't get too caught up in specific goals. It's all okay as long as you keep moving in the right direction. The next section looks at the difference between goals and values in more detail and explains why following values means not getting attached too firmly to specific goals, however virtuous they may be.

FOLLOWING VALUES – THE LIFE OF TWISTS AND TURNS

Think of the way a river flows to the ocean. It always flows downwards. Guided by its value *downwards* it gets to the ocean (its final and ultimate purpose), but it sure isn't following a straight line. A river cannot set its direction by a particular tree, or by a certain house, or any other thing that happens to lie straight ahead of it on a direct line to the ocean as the crow flies, because straight ahead can be away from its value of *downwards*. Always it flows downhill, but there are many meanders, many twists and turns in the river as the water flows around obstacles, around hills and rocks in its path. Sometimes the river even seems to be moving away from the ocean, but only if your thinking is flat or two-dimensional, if distance is measured just in miles or kilometres away from the ocean. Measured in *downwardness*, in metres above sea level, the water is always getting closer to the ocean. It turns away from a goal that seems to be where it was heading because it is following its value, it isn't being thrown off course at all, and it will reach the ocean because it does turn. It is because it turns, because it adjusts its heading, that it doesn't get stuck. So it is with us when we are following our values. Because we don't get to control all the obstacles on the path, we often need to change our expectations of where we thought we were going, or what we thought we would be doing. We may have to take our sights off any particular goal we thought was on the way and adjust our aim when circumstances change. When we hit an obstacle or barrier or sudden drop, our values may dictate a course change. Twisting and turning in these circumstances is actually staying on track.

It may be a good thing to set a routine and not waste time, to have a goal of mowing the lawn today, but not if it means we can't make space to help another, not if we can't let go of the lawn mowing when our neighbour needs a ride to the hospital. We may have had a plan to finish writing our thesis, weed the garden, or wrap our Christmas gifts today, but following values may dictate that all these goals be abandoned if a friend needs someone to talk to.

So stay flexible, any goal you set for yourself should be set with a *contingency*, with an *out clause*, or by appending a *God willing,* for following your values may lead you away from the goal you set. This was the lesson Henry van Dyke sought to express in his beautiful novella *The Story of the Other Wise Man* published in 1895. The novella tells the story of a fourth wise man who never made it to Nazareth to see the baby Jesus and worship him there, because of doing good deeds all along the way until it was too late. The message is that in doing these deeds and acting on values of love and compassion, he was worshiping Jesus though not in the way he planned, and not by achieving the original goal he set.

You can't use rules to keep you on track to values. Actions have to be held up against values and not rules. It might be good to avoid confrontations, it might be good to save money, it might be good to go to bed early, but none of these good ideas should be allowed to become hard and fast rules with the power to block your path towards values. Rule-following can go too far. It can become an easy and a lazy mental substitute for engagement in analysis, in spending time with moral dilemmas. People use rules to avoid any sense of guilt or responsibility for their choices. Just apply the rule and whatever happens, happens; we're not to blame!

Rule-following can lead a person away from values when circumstances are not considered. The truth is, a person is not free, but is instead a slave to rules, if rules and not values determine their actions. Jesus had to be free to heal on the Sabbath.

SELF-CONTROL IS FREEDOM

As previously quoted Austrian 18th Century writer Marie von Ebner-Eschenbach said:

> As far as your self-control goes, as far goes your freedom.

Self-control is the path to true freedom because true freedom means to be unrestrained in our choice to follow our values. Freedom means being able to become the person we want to be. It is not freedom to be pulled off course by errors of judgment or to be controlled by emotion or thought. Self-control, also called self-discipline, means using and strengthening one's executive function, by saying no to impulses to act in ways that do not align with our values.

This sort of freedom is not freedom from the existence of difficult thoughts and feelings or temptations, instead, it is freedom to act as one chooses. A person who has self-control can act as they choose not as their emotions suggest. Their actions are free. Think of it like this: if you are 'free' of prison, it does not necessarily follow or require that prisons do not exist, only that you are not confined in a prison. In the same way, values free you from difficult or painful thoughts and feelings. Painful thoughts and feelings continue to exist, yes, but they do not constrain you. You are out of prison, you are free.

Self-control therefore means being free to be your own best self, released from bondage to pleasure or pain, from ambition and the desires of others. It means freedom to pursue the values of your inner heart. Freedom to pursue true happiness. To seek the things that matter most. To be free means that every day you live has the chance to become the most beautiful day of your life.

To quote Paul Dubois:

> The sole liberty that man enjoys is the power to react under the influence of an idea, the ability to obey either the motive of feeling, that is to say of his passions or the motives of reason.

and

> Self-control is acquired only by a constant reflection; it rests upon a clear view of moral determinism which by making men equal creates true humility. For control demands indulgence for others linked to severity towards self, courage in the struggle against the passions, and moderation even in the legitimate pleasures, to which we may be led.

The more you give in to your emotions and let them take control of you and your actions, the stronger they get, overall, and each one individually, and the less free you will be. Of course, you can choose to go punch a punching bag to let out anger, no one is harmed and it may even align with your value of getting fitter or stronger as part of self-care, but not so if you lose control and punch the person who has made you angry. The more small angers and fears you prevent from taking charge of you, from making you act in ways that do not align with your values, the more able you will be to resist stronger anger, fear and grief when larger trials come. Always remember that when we lose control of ourselves, when we move away from our values, we are moving away from ourselves as we want to be. We are moving away from our idealised vision of humanity.

The key to self-control is always to stop and think before you respond to an event. This applies just as much to events in the mind, as it does to events in the world. Allow time to evaluate a situation before choosing what to do. Slow down. There is always a tiny space between event and reaction, a space in which you can pause and choose how to respond (unless it is a true reflex like your knee jumping when it's hit with a tendon hammer!) Once we acknowledge that there is a gap between impulse and action, however small, we can widen it. We can stop and establish self-control at the point between impulse, which is not under your conscious control, and reaction, which is. So, don't let emotions or thoughts take charge and steer you off course.

If you need to make more space in which reason can act, jam your foot in the door to make more space. Breathe. Count to

10, or 100! Sleep on it. Go for a walk. Give your slower reasoning brain time to analyse the situation.

KINDNESS – THE ALL-EMBRACING VALUE

The following few sections present a few thoughts on individual values. Certainly it doesn't cover all of them, I haven't written sections on hospitality, humour, loyalty or generosity. The door is open to you to select the words that represent most closely what you value most in others and so value the most in yourself.

I will start my thoughts with kindness because kindness is the master value. Like a master key, kindness unlocks all the rest of the values. This is because to be kind is to be tolerant, to be kind is to be patient, to be kind is to have empathy, to be supportive, to be reliable, honest, forgiving, respectful, encouraging, loyal, courageous, interested, tactful, empowering, trustworthy, generous, constant in action, grateful, etc. All virtues are held within kindness.

Many are the thinkers who have recognised and taught the supremacy of kindness, compassion or love above all other values. What follows is a quote from Paul Dubois in which he reflects on the one value we truly need, which of course is kindness, and the nature of values as guides to life in general.

> There is nobody in the world, however disinherited he may be, who has not experienced the benefit of kindness from a mother, a friend or some person or other, perhaps only that

of a faithful dog. From the minute he has the conception of that virtue it is easy for him to imagine somebody better than his benefactor, and beyond that another, still a better one. This "always better" leads us straight to infinity, to the idea of kindness. In the same way, we conceive the idea of other virtues, whose beauty we recognise and it is this gathered knowledge that will make the beacon of our ideal. Also we often allow this beacon to go out, which we should so carefully preserve, and render brighter by adding the ideal of another virtue! There are virtues whose beauty we do not immediately recognise, thus humility is very little appreciated and chastity is ridiculed. It needs a certain maturity of mind to arrive at patience and tolerance; these are not the virtues of youth. The great fault of man is to lower his ideal, while it can never be placed too high. It is not a goal within our reach, it is a star in the firmament that guides our feet. Doubtless we often go astray, but it is always there, and so we should look up! Do not become discouraged, and to make the task easier, do not take an object nearer us as guide, a will-o'-the-wisp which is disappearing, the light of a house about to be put out, a traveller who does not know the way.

Our innate emotional responses are in most cases enough to make us mother our baby, or defend our home and family, just as a tigress cares for her kittens, or a silverback gorilla defends his troop. Behaviours that are instinctive, or in other words, innate, biological and shared with other species, therefore are not clear evidence of compassion. So what then does universal love or compassion mean? It means expanding the experience of family love to include the ones whom your emotional brain sees as *other*, those for whom it generates no instinctual love. Many religious and philosophical teachings attempt to widen the instinctive love we have for our closest kin in wide arcs, arcs which aspire to encompass the whole world. This is likely to seem "pie in the sky" to many readers, but, we, as modern people, interact with many people outside our own family or tribe in a typical day. We cannot act towards them with the instinctive hostility and suspicion strangers met with from our hunter-gatherer ancestors. To heal the world, we need to at least aspire to a philosophy of love.

To again quote my favourite French-Swiss doctor Paul Dubois:

> There is no virtue, to speak correctly, for man as a solitary individual in the world. Virtue begins only with sociability. All our qualities have their reverberations upon the happiness of our fellow men; they enjoy them, as we enjoy theirs. The idea of responsibility is at the base of all our aspirations towards good.

> True kindness is more clear-sighted. It is only established slowly in human understanding, it grows with moral intelligence, with self-control. It is the fruit of that meditative thought which, by analyzing the elements of happiness, induces us to seek it, not in the material advantages offered to our appetites, like bait to foolish fish, but in the pursuit of a fine ideal useful to others and to ourselves.

That is why I consider as one of the simplest dicta of reason the idea that we must not do to others what we do not wish them to do to us......There is continual indecision in our conduct when we have not sufficiently recognised the necessity for an ideal, or when we have not placed it high enough.

and Marie von Ebner-Eschenbach:

How wise must one be to be always kind.

Kindness includes kindness towards oneself, self-kindness is demonstrated in the way we care for our emotional self and our physical body.

Why don't you see if you can give yourself a gift, a life-enhancing and pleasant one? It could be a massage or a new pair of running shoes. It could be a walk around the garden. It could be an afternoon listening to music or with your favourite book. Give it to yourself in love, respect and kind-ness, and accept it with gratitude and thankfulness. Allow yourself to take pleasure in giving and in receiving a gift from yourself.

AUTHENTICITY

There is a school of thought that argues we should act just as we feel. Certainly, we should never feign emotions such as friendship, love or admiration, in order to take advantage of others. But that does not mean we should let our inner emotional brain take control of the steering wheel of our lives. To suggest it is inauthentic to do good unless you feel like it is quite wrong. Think about it and you will see that the opposite is true.

Courageous acts are *more* and not *less* courageous when undertaken without feeling brave, acts of love or kindness are more kind and more loving when done to help a stranger than done for a close friend or family member. We show greater generosity when we give of ourselves, sacrificing our time or sharing things we could use ourselves than when we share things we don't want, the things we feel like giving, the leftovers of our time and resources.

Remember feelings are unstable, they change constantly, they are unreliable, variable as clouds in the sky or waves on the surface of the sea. To be guided by feelings is to be erratic, unpredictable and unreliable. With emotions in charge, your bus will be all over the road. It is also a bad idea to rely on thoughts to guide you. Imagine watching a movie instead of the road when you are driving! Let reality guide you and keep flights of fancy to times when it's okay to daydream. There's a good reason we don't do the things we think we're doing when we are asleep and dreaming!

Examine your inner emotional core and your verbal mind and you will soon see their inconstancy. You may feel kind towards someone today and feel harsh towards them tomorrow. You felt enthused yesterday; today you don't feel like doing anything. But the value of moving in the right direction is still in place. If you follow either your emotions or your thoughts uncritically, your boat will not reach home port. So, do not set sail through life by these phantoms, but instead by the guiding light of values. Live a life of constancy. Be trustworthy and steadfast.

We show who we are, our authentic selves, and what matters to us, by doing what is right when we don't feel like it, more than we show our values and who we are by the good we do others and ourselves when we feel like it.

POSITIVITY

William James, sometimes referred to as the father of American psychology, wrote in his book *Talks to Teachers on Psychology and to Students on some of Life's Ideals* (James, 1899) the following:

> Actions seem to follow feeling, but really actions and feeling go together; and by regulating the action, which is under the more direct control of the will, we can indirectly regulate the feeling, which is not.

> Thus the sovereign voluntary path to cheerfulness, if your cheerfulness be lost, is to sit up cheerfully and to act and speak as if cheerfulness were already there.

So, put on a smile and let its happiness sink in, or sing a song to cheer your heart.

COURAGE

Sometimes you need a pair of pliers to open a jar, sometimes the lid comes off easily. In much the same way you may not need courage to accomplish every value-directed action you choose, but it often does take courage to act based on values. Like patience, courage is a value to keep close at hand.

Many people avoid stress and discomfort by withdrawing from painful situations or ones of conflict, by leaving jobs, avoiding neighbours, etc., and as long as this avoidance doesn't take you away from your values, there is no problem with that. But there are times when values will lead you into pain, and away from pleasure. There are times when there is no turning away from suffering and pain that is compatible with love, and we certainly need courage with us then. For example, to avoid contact with a suffering loved one is to be more concerned with our feelings of discomfort than with the one we love. We may love them, but we don't love them enough, not if we love our comfort more. Second century AD Stoic philosopher and teacher Epictetus used a story about a father who ran from his daughter's sick bed to illustrate this point. The lesson was recorded by his student Arrian in *The Enchiridion*.

We also need courage to stick to our convictions in the face of censure from others. It does not always make one popular to do what is right, for example, to speak unwelcome truths. You should not expect others to admire you or like you because you adhere to your values, but you can expect to admire and like yourself, which is more important.

To quote Paul Dubois on courage:

> One often needs it in order to express frankly a thought
> that one has matured, to do it without fear of conflicting
> with that of others, to have, as we say the courage of our
> opinion. How cowardly men are upon this point! One sees
> believers putting their banners in their pockets...

MODERATION

Aristotle, a Greek philosopher who lived in the 4th Century
BC, considered virtues to be the golden mean between two
opposing vices. For example, *determination* is the mean
between pig-headedness and spinelessness. *Courage* can be
seen as the mean between recklessness and cowardice. The
point is that anything, even a virtue, taken too far turns into
a vice. Economy becomes miserliness, self-reliance becomes
arrogance and pride. The concept is also reflected in both
Jewish and Christian teaching. Consider this verse from the
first testament book of Ecclesiastes 7:18. New International
Version:

> Whoever fears God will avoid all extremes.

Excess has no moral value. Do not mortify yourself, squat on
a pole for years, starve yourself or engage in other extremes,
that is not virtue but foolishness.

GRATITUDE

Everyone likes to be thanked. Even Jesus complained that only one of a group of ten healed lepers returned to say thank you (Luke 17:11-18. New International Version):

> Now on his way to Jerusalem, Jesus travelled along the border between Samaria and Galilee. As he was going into a village, ten men who had leprosy met him. They stood at a distance and called out in a loud voice, "Jesus, Master, have pity on us!" When he saw them, he said, "Go, show your-selves to the priests." And as they went, they were cleansed. One of them, when he saw he was healed, came back, praising God in a loud voice. He threw himself at Jesus' feet and thanked him—and he was a Samaritan. Jesus asked, "Were not all ten cleansed? Where are the other nine? Has no one returned to give praise to God except this foreigner?"

I do not doubt that all ten lepers were extremely grateful for their healing from what is a truly vile disease, but Jesus expresses the very human longing for gratitude. So let us see if we can try to show gratitude openly for the good that others do for us, at least sometimes. I offer a quote from Albert Schweitzer's *Memoirs of Childhood and Youth* (Schweitzer, 1956):

> We ought all to make an effort to act on our first thoughts and let our unspoken gratitude find expression. Then there will be more sunshine in the world, and more power to

work for what is good. But as concerns ourselves we must all of us take care not to adopt as part of our theory of life all people's bitter sayings about the ingratitude of the world. A great deal of water is flowing underground which never comes up as a spring. In that thought we may find comfort. But we ourselves must try to be the water which does find its way up; we must become a spring at which men can quench their thirst for gratitude.

HOPE

Let's start a discussion of hope with a quote from "The Aeneid" by Virgil written between 29 and 19 BC:

> *Fortune has played with many a man and set him free again.*

The message is: Do not lose hope. Things can get better.

Musonius Rufus, who was the leader of the Stoic school of philosophy in Rome in the first century AD, said:

> And if you choose to hold fast to what is right, do not be irked by difficult circumstances, but reflect on how many things have already happened to you in life in ways that you did not wish, and yet they have turned out for the best.

And from St Paul, Romans 8:28. New Living Translation:

And we know that God causes everything to work together for the good of those who love God and are called according to his purpose for them.

As said by Maria quoting the Reverend Mother in the 1965 classic movie *The Sound of Music*:

When the Lord closes a door, somewhere he opens a window.

So don't stand for long in front of a closed door, look around for the open window, for a new opportunity. Remember hope is one of three things that St Paul said go on forever (1 Corinthians 13:13). You can create your own hope by anticipation of a future pleasant event, like a visit to or from a friend, a sight-seeing trip, a new book from your favourite author due for release this year or a new series of your favourite TV show.... As long as it is in line with your values, it's okay to have something to look forward to.

DIVERSITY

Why do people like uniformity? Why do we want to see dancers all making the same moves, homogeneous marching girls, book spines all lined up, etc? People vary in how much they are attracted to sameness, as they do in every other thing, but we all like to hear the voices of a choir joined as one.

Nature is full of diversity. There are many flower shapes, many different coloured fish, many different forms and consistencies of leaves, so many kinds of any kind of thing that is. There is no kind of anything which human eyes can see, for which each one is the same, not clouds, not snowflakes, not cats, not dogs, not hens, not blades of grass, and all of us humans too are unique, with a unique story and a unique way of looking at the world. We need to value diversity more, and when we do, we will be better equipped to tolerate difference. I was sad when I heard that the Chinese Communist Party selected women of the same age (18–24 years) height (168–178 cm), weight, width of nose, length of face and even slant of eyes, along with the ability to show exactly eight teeth when they smiled, to be 2008 Beijing Olympic hostesses. If we learn to value diversity and uniqueness more than we do, it will help us to value ourselves and others more highly. Why don't we try to see every one of us as a unique work of divine art?

HONESTY

Pretty much everyone agrees honesty is a good idea and has for a long time. The legal text or code, composed from 1755 to 1750 BC by Babylonian King Hammurabi, specified the death penalty for those bearing false witness in court or stealing property. Honesty is vital to healthy relationships, successful business, good government, industry and science. Truth is to be preferred; truth is the basis of civilization. Lies told by doctors, scientists, priests, politicians, advertisers, fraudsters, thieves and unfaithful spouses, told for personal advantage and heedless of effects on others, are surely evil.

So, instead of singing the praises of honesty, I have decided to give you a few thoughts about when and why it might be *right* to lie.

Is it ever right to lie? Or even one's duty to lie? If so, when? This is a situation of values conflict, or a moral dilemma, where, like the morality of violence in self-defence, or the characteristics of a just war, a behaviour generally seen as immoral, such as lying, may be morally acceptable.

My answer is this. It is moral to lie and practice deception to prevent harm in the face of the abuse of power. In other words, it is right to lie in a situation where someone with power over you is doing evil, is causing harm, and you have no other prudent way to prevent it. In such cases lying is resistance to tyranny.

Could it ever be your moral duty to lie? Sometimes the motivation to lie is advantage to someone else, and to lie will not offer any advantage to us but instead will incur great personal risk. Those are times we may have a duty to lie but few would have the courage to do it. An explanatory example would be lying to the Gestapo about the whereabouts of a Jew when one is not oneself Jewish. Acting on moral absolutisms like, "You must never lie," would in this situation be an example of destructive rule-following and not one of responsibility to values.

It hardly needs to be said that lying is never right in the service of evil, not right for material advantage, not right to hide one's previous immoral behaviour or to harm others. Lying can only be right as a mitigating response to the evil of those in power. Such were the lies of Christian Martyr Dietrich Bonhoeffer during his involvement with a plot to assassinate Hitler. Other examples of this type of moral lying are the lies of the biblical midwives Shiphrah and Puah as recorded in Exodus Chapter 1. On being ordered by Pharaoh to kill all newborn Hebrew male infants as they delivered them, these brave midwives told Pharaoh the lie that Hebrew women give birth quickly, in fact before a midwife can arrive (Exodus 1:15-19. New International Version):

> The king of Egypt said to the Hebrew midwives, whose names were Shiphrah and Puah, "When you are helping the Hebrew women during childbirth on the delivery stool, if you see that the baby is a boy, kill him; but if it is a girl, let her live." The midwives, however, feared God and did not do what the king of Egypt had told them to do; they let the boys live. Then the king of Egypt summoned the midwives and asked them, "Why have you done this? Why have you let the boys live?" The midwives answered Pharaoh, "Hebrew women are not like Egyptian women; they are vigorous and give birth before the midwives arrive."

This is a quite different kind of moral lying from the "white lies" we are all so fond of, and which are widely considered morally neutral. So what of those petty lies of conversation, the things we say to flatter and amuse, to foster friendships, etc? Are these white lies ok? Are they morally neutral or not? Are they are intended to advantage the liar, not the receiver of the white lie? Before we tell such lies, we should ask ourselves if these white lies are really for another's benefit, or if in fact they for our own personal advantage, to make someone like us or to facilitate some personal gain? If so, they are not really "white lies" are they? And even if we do not seek some advantage, we should seriously consider how much value we place on honesty before turning away from it like a dandelion seed tossing in the breeze. Is any small advantage worth sacrificing honesty? If you want to encourage someone and say something nice, it isn't hard to find something true to say.

To summarise my view: it is morally right to lie when someone has power over you or someone else and is abusing that power to cause severe harm or threat to life, and you have no safe recourse to other means of redress. It may even be a duty to lie when the harm prevented is to another and not oneself. In other words, a lie can only be moral in the presence of evil. Marcus Aurelius said we should never lie, but he was a Roman Emperor, a man in a position of great power who was never held hostage in the power of a tyrant.

HUMILITY

If you choose not to behave as other people around you do, some may consider you self-righteous. Their interpretations are not in your control. You cannot stop others from forming opinions. But do not let them be right about it!

What is self-righteousness? It means to be self-satisfied, to be proud, confident and puffed up in your estimation of your virtue, forgetting that you still have a long way to go and fall far short of the target. It means comparing yourself favourably to others, and worse to make that comparison public, letting others know that you think you are better than they are. You are not better than they are. The truth is that if you were them, were in their situation, and had had their experiences, you would be thinking and acting just as they are.

Do not be like the Pharisee described in Luke 18:9-14. New International Version:

> To some who were confident of their own righteousness and looked down on everyone else, Jesus told this parable: "Two men went up to the temple to pray, one a Pharisee and the other a tax collector. The Pharisee stood by himself and prayed: 'God, I thank you that I am not like other people—robbers, evildoers, adulterers—or even like this tax collector. I fast twice a week and give a tenth of all I get.'"

Do not think too much of yourself and your abilities. You are special, yes, but no more so than any other of the more than eight billion humans currently living. You are not perfect and you never will be. You always stay a work in progress. If you are making steady progress towards living in accord with your values, you are doing well.

Paul Dubois on humility:

For all those who have not to strive for worldly success, there is a better means of lessening timidity; it is to suppress self-love, the wish to be appreciated for ones' self. One then disappears behind the task one undertakes. We may still have qualms on the possibility of accomplishing it but our person is not in question, we no longer bring up the idle and always dangerous question "How shall I look?"

We only arrive at this impersonal view which shields us from timidity through true humility. Forgetfulness of ourselves enables us to kindle enthusiasm for a cause, to become an apostle for it.

There is another important aspect to humility, which is not being too proud to accept help. We all need help from time to time or often. Don't be too proud to admit you need other people. Accept help when offered with humility and gratitude. Pride is, however, not the only reason people refuse help. There are other reasons, for example, fear of incurring debt or obligation, of owing someone something, or even of maybe one day being asked to repay. I have known people to refuse an invitation to eat at someone's home, not because they didn't want to go, but because they would not be able to return the invitation in kind. To be humble is to be willing to accept gifts of kindness and generosity from others. When we give help because it is our value to do so, then that good deed is its own reward, we do not expect anything back. The same applies in reverse. Where help is offered freely, where it is offered for kindness, for support, etc., you are free to accept it without incurring obligation. Of course, this does not apply if you have entered into a contract to pay someone back, if the help was purchased and not freely given. But if it is a gift, accept it, and don't worry if you can never pay the kindness back. We need to move beyond a *you scratch my back and I'll scratch yours* attitude, and instead be willing to pay it forward. I will do what I can for you, and you will do what you can for someone else. Being willing to both give, and receive help, without any expectation of return, will keep the wheels of care spinning, and that is after all the reason we are here: to help one another.

A COMMENT ON FORGIVENESS

This section has been kept short because a long reflection on forgiveness from a Christian perspective is included in Chapter 7: Spiritual help for living – How faith can help you be happy.

Remember two wrongs don't make a right. Negative one plus negative one is negative two, not zero. Make no mistake in the algebra of values!

In 1711, 22-year-old English poet Alexander Pope wrote:

To err is human; to forgive, divine.

Ephesians 4:32. New International Version:

Be kind and compassionate to one another, forgiving each other, just as in Christ God forgave you.

Marie von Ebner-Eschenbach said:

> We should always forgive. We should forgive the repentant
> for their sake, the unrepentant for our sake.

RELIABILITY

Are you a person others can rely on when they need support? Can you be relied on to give a helping hand when you're asked? Are you a bridge over troubled water for others? Do you provide others with a place of safety, with a place to shelter from the storm? Does your presence in any distressing or difficult situation provide others with a stepping stone, or are you a stumbling stone whose presence makes bad things worse?

Let's think about a question for a moment. What makes a stone a thing for stumbling over, to steer clear of, and what instead makes it a stepping stone, a place of attraction, of invitation and a promise of safety? Stepping stones are predictable, reliable and trustworthy. They inspire confidence. They lie low to the ground, never presenting an obstacle to a traveller's progress. Stumbling stones, on the other hand, come in two varieties. One kind looks okay, but moves in unpredictable ways, shifting under people's feet and upsetting their balance, so that they stumble and fall. The second kind of stumbling stone blocks people's way, forcing them off course onto rougher ground, where they may stumble or lose their way.

Being reliable means being a stepping stone, not either kind of stumbling stone.

TOLERANCE AND NOT JUDGING OTHERS

Quote from *The Enchiridion* on refraining from judging others:

> Someone bathes in haste, don't say he bathes badly but in haste, someone drinks a lot of wine, don't say he drinks badly but a lot. Until you know their reasons, how do you know their actions are vicious? This will save you from perceiving one thing clearly but then assenting to something different.

In other words, stick to the facts rather than adding your opinion.

Instead of rushing to judgment if someone has done you wrong, consider if there is another way to interpret the situation, one that casts a gentler light on their actions. Your spouse yelled at you? Instead of being upset, consider, for example, the possibility they have had a hard day. Generally, there is another way to get a handle on any situation, one that is more balanced and more useful.

Don't make judgments personal. Judge actions separately from the person doing the action. For example, talk of dishonest actions, not dishonest people.

Especially do not criticize others or look down on them for anything over which they have no control, such as their race, sex, place of birth, height, age, parents, etc., and don't judge yourself either on any of these things. You have no reason to be proud that you were dealt a better hand by chance or fate or birth. You're not a more humane person because you're more intelligent, because you're taller, stronger or any of the things you gained *gratis* as a result of the genetic lottery.

Remember no one is perfect and that includes you. As recounted in the Gospel of John chapter 8, when Jesus wanted to stop an angry crowd from stoning a woman, he told them that whoever was without sin, should throw the first stone. Jesus knew no one would throw a stone, for if anyone had, the crowd would have turned on them for their hypocrisy. We all know no one is without sin. We are all flawed people living with other flawed people, and so we need to be tolerant of each other.

Paul Dubois said the following about what sustained him in avoiding making harsh judgements of the unhelpful choices he saw his patients make:

> We constantly forget that the persons talking to us think with the heads that are upon their shoulders and not with our heads, that they see things from another angle, in other colours. We forget that we should think as they do if we had the same temperament, if we had experienced the same educational, physical, intellectual and moral influences.... Has not St Francis de Sales said, "Better silence a truth than give it ungently and with bad grace!"

Men are always, at the time we observe them, what they are able to be; let us forgive them and provide them with the means to reach the goal with greater chances of success.

We too can avoid judging others by understanding they are doing their best.

PRUDENCE (PRACTICAL WISDOM)

Prudence is wisdom is knowing the difference between the things that one should be able to do, and what one should do! It is the virtue of common sense also called *street smarts*. Prudence means remembering this is the real world, the world in which bad things happen. The world is the way it is. It's not the way you or anyone else thinks it should be. Prudence acknowledges the reality of the world we live in. Life is a difficult and dangerous place. Practical wisdom means taking wise actions based on the way the world is. We can have ideals, in fact we must have them, but we should not be idealistic fools!

It is not wise to confuse how we want the world to be, with how the universe is. It is not wise to assume people are how we would like them to be. Everyone should be honest, but it's a fool who believes everything they are told! It should be safe to leave our cars unlocked while we duck into grocery stores, and the doors of our houses open at night, but it would be reckless to do so.

A focus on reality, on what is instead of what is not, is essential to choosing prudent actions. Prudence is doing the wise thing in a particular situation. It is asking, before taking any particular action, what, if any, are the risks of taking this action, and then considering if it is reasonable to take those risks?

Do not be offended by common sense. It is not victim blaming to recommend prudence, to advise on how one might reduce one's chances of becoming a victim, or to call attention to the way life and other people are. Of course, we want the world to be better, and we should do our best to work towards a situation where there is not such a wide divide between what one should be able to do, and what one actually should do. But while the divide exists, and that may be forever, it will stay prudent advice to tell a young woman, "Hitchhiking on your own isn't a good idea."

SELF-CARE

Self-harm includes taking drugs of abuse, cutting oneself, starving oneself, heavy drinking and any other physically damaging behaviour. Even if a self-harm behaviour produces a temporary sense of pleasure (first happiness), or gets attention from others, any behaviour you don't admire in others you won't admire in yourself. Behaving in ways you don't admire, ways that do not align with your values, will make you feel less like a person who deserves care, less like a person who deserves love in your own eyes. That is how self-destructive behaviours make you feel worse about yourself. They lower your self-esteem. When your self-esteem is low, it is harder to find the self-love and compassion needed to resist the urge to self-harm. In this way self-harming behaviour reinforces itself and becomes yet another example of a vicious cycle. You can't feel better about yourself by hurting yourself.

This means that the best way to overcome the urge to self-harm is to lean into your values. If you start to feel good about your kindness, your patience, your courage, your resilience, your common sense, your flexibility, etc., then you will like yourself more. As you start to care about yourself more and more, you will not want to put yourself in harm's way. Self-love and self-compassion will be restored along with your self-esteem.

Whatever you think of yourself right now, you are a human person, a person capable of evaluating thoughts and feelings, capable of making choices. God loves you and doesn't want to see you hurt. If you think you are not worth anything, that you deserve pain, can you do something kind for yourself because that would please God? Draw a line in the sand. This line is *now*, it separates the past from the future. Leave self-harm behind as you step over that line, as you step out and away from the time of harm into the time of healing.

AVOIDING TEMPTATION

There may be times when it's wise to avoid something, not because the thing is in itself a move away from values, but because it increases our risk of making such a move. If we understand that we all have our weaknesses, that we are human, and that at least for now, our self-control is not up to the task, we won't put too much temptation in our way. If, for example, we have decided not to drink, maybe we should stay out of pubs. If we wish not to gamble, we should probably stay away from casinos, etc. You can't avoid a pitfall or other obstacle if you won't acknowledge it's there. The point is to not overestimate our ability to act the way we want to in every situation. It takes time to learn to live in accord with values. Acknowledging and owning our weaknesses is a helpful first step. Be humble about your weaknesses. Don't get into a fight with temptations stronger than yourself. Over time, as our self-control grows, old habits lose their appeal and perhaps we won't need to avoid places, where, for the sake of our examples, drinking or gambling are going on. Until then, the prudent thing to do is to avoid even the risk of temptation.

*navigating
the rapids*

SEE CHANGE AS GROWTH

Try to remember that being changed is not the same as being damaged. A caterpillar has to change to become a butterfly, a process in which its old body is first destroyed. Suffering changes people, but that change is not always a harm, it can be an improvement. A raw gemstone needs to have its rough edges polished off to make it shine. Think of a leadlight window. A leadlight window is more beautiful, it is more intricate than a plain glass window that was never broken. The lead seams create the design. They create the beauty. A patchwork quilt can be exquisite. So it can be with a broken heart when splendid seams of healing become art.

Breaking things and then putting them back together can also make them stronger than what they were made of.

Think of aggregate bench tops or laminated wood. These are many times less brittle than their raw source material.

American poet Mary Oliver wrote in her poem "The Uses of Sorrow" a line which reads:

> *Someone I loved once gave me*
> *a box full of darkness.*
>
> *It took me years to understand*
> *that this too was a gift.*

Living into post-traumatic growth is made easier if you accept that suffering creates the conditions under which a person can grow in humanity. Pain can be transformed by love into something of value, as if you could really do, what the miller said his pretty daughter could, that is, spin straw into gold.

Whether broken things come back together more beautiful and stronger than before, or do not, depends on how that putting back together is done. For something good, something strong, something beautiful to emerge out of what was broken, the putting back together needs to be done with purpose and design. Love needs to guide that process. Perhaps you can use what you have learnt to bring healing to others. How are you a better person than you were before? For what have you been trained? What is the work for which you are now uniquely qualified?

It may be helpful to meditate on the words of St Paul recorded in his letter to the Romans (Romans 8:28. King James Version):

> And we know that all things work together for good to them that love God, to them who are the called according to his purpose.

The same concept of adversity turning into benefit was present in Stoic thought recorded during a similar period to the development of Christianity.

A quote from *Meditations*:

> Just as nature takes every obstacle, every impediment, and works around it – turns it to its purposes, incorporates it into itself – so, too, a rational being can turn each setback into raw material and use it to achieve its goal.

The story of Joseph, as recorded in the Book of Genesis, is another tale of good coming out of evil. Joseph was sold by his brothers and taken to Egypt as a slave. Sounds bad right? But not so fast, for in Egypt Joseph rises to become a powerful administrator in a position to help his family, including his treacherous brothers, during a famine. The Bible records what Joseph told his brothers when they came asking for help (Genesis 4:5. New King James Version):

> But now, do not therefore be grieved or angry with your-

selves because you sold me here; for God sent me before
you to preserve life.

Genesis 50:19-21. New International Version:

But Joseph said to them, "Don't be afraid. Am I in the place
of God? You intended to harm me, but God intended it for
good to accomplish what is now being done, the saving of
many lives. So then, don't be afraid. I will provide for you
and your children." And he reassured them and spoke
kindly to them.

PRACTICE MAKES PERFECT

Our brains change to get better and better at the things we
do most often. New ways of thinking and acting create new
connections and pathways in your brain, until, things that
once seemed hard seem natural and the only way to be. This
is neuroplasticity at work. The more you practice something
difficult, the easier it gets. In time, maintaining self-control
and following your values will get easier, just like riding a
bike, driving a car or walking tightropes gets easier. And it
may even start to look easy to others, but like any tightrope
walker, you will know that it is never exactly easy! The truth
is there will always be a certain amount of challenge, and
sometimes a lot in staying your course. It is never totally
automatic and there will be many falls, bumps, wobbles and
serves along the way. Praise yourself for your efforts.

CRITIQUE COMPLAINING

Do you like hearing others complain? Does it feel as if they expect you to fix a problem they should solve themselves, or that can't be solved? Or that they would rather complain than take the good advice you offer in response?

How do others react when you complain? Do they say things like, "Why are you telling me about it? That's not my problem. What do you expect me to do about it? Quit complaining, whining, whinging, etc." The truth is that complaints annoy others and so like other human behaviours that upset or annoy other people, complaining has become one of the many stars available for psychiatry's link-the-dots manual of disorders, the Diagnostic and Statistical Manual or DSM. Excessive complaining is listed as a symptom of depression, and more than one personality disorder.

Babies have to complain. They have no independent way to get their needs met. But before we complain, at least more than once about any one thing, to any one person, we might well consider the following. Can we simply get what we want for ourselves? Is the other person in a position to help or not? And just as important, if we would be willing to allow them to help us if they offered to?

Does it get you anywhere to complain about things that can't be fixed? To be given advice you don't want to follow? Does it make you feel better or worse? And how does being complained at about things you have no way to address, or having your help refused make you feel?

The short answer is that complaining when help is not available, or won't be accepted, creates misery and resentment, reinforcing the pathways of unpleasant emotion in the brains of both the complainer and the one being complained to. So, while it is fine to express our unhappiness about any particular situation and event, we are well advised to limit repeated complaining to situations where it has some chance of leading to the meeting of our needs. Otherwise, our happiness, as well as the happiness of others, is better served by finding things to be grateful for instead. Gratitude journals, counting your blessings and expressing gratitude to and for others, are useful ways to improve our and other people's mood.

STOP CARING SO MUCH ABOUT WHAT OTHERS THINK

Cynic philosophy, which predated Stoicism, and in which Stoicism had its roots, included the tenet that we should practice not being ashamed of things which are not the result of our own poor choices. Cynics, just as their descendants the Stoics did, that a person should never be ashamed of their family of origin, their race, their height, their sex, their age, any illness or disfigurement they may have, nor anything any other person ever did or said to or about them. Just as one should not be proud of the things one was merely given in the lottery of life; one should not be ashamed of such things either. Pride and shame alike should be reserved for our own choices to behave with virtue or with vice.

Let others think what they may. Our job is to attend to our most important task, the pursuit of true lasting happiness, which means aligning our actions with our values. The praise of people you do not admire for their moral character is of little value. They are most likely to praise you for doing what they do and living as they do. Criticism from others, on the other hand, may be of value. To quote Stoic Philosopher Seneca, who was active in Rome in the first century AD:

> A good man delights in receiving advice. All the worse men are the most impatient of guidance.

If we are criticised, we can try to remember that we are none of us perfect after all, and so criticism should not be dismissed outright, it should be considered in order to see if it may be helpful to us in some way.

ALLOW OTHER PEOPLE TO BE WRONG

Jesus himself could not lead everyone to see things his way. Jesus experienced rejection as recorded in several gospel accounts. Why should we expect that we will do better? "The Parable of the Sower" teaches that however good a seed is, however true the message, if it falls on infertile ground it will not grow.

In an older story, recorded in the Hebrew Scriptures, Jonah was asked to deliver God's call for repentance to the people of the city of Nineveh. He was not to be responsible for making the people repent, only for delivering the message.

Likewise, we cannot be responsible for other people's decisions for we are not in charge of other people. Some people will insist that black is white, that two and two are five. If so, move on. Be satisfied to be right without needing to prove others wrong, or getting them to admit their errors.

Sometimes while the disagreement relates to a matter of fact, the facts cannot be verified at least not at the current time. In these cases, agree to disagree. Remember, your opinion about what is, or what happened, may be the one that does align with reality, or maybe it is instead you that is wrong about whether there is life on other planets or if the dog your parent's neighbours had when you were ten was called Rover or Rider. Being willing to agree to disagree is even more relevant when it is not facts that are involved, but matters of opinion, matters of politics, of taste or religion.

DEALING WITH DIFFICULT PEOPLE

It is especially important to keep your values in mind when dealing with difficult people. I am not talking here about abusive people, I am talking about difficult people, particularly family members, who are going to stay part of your life. If you find it difficult or stressful to interact with someone close to you, because of past difficulties or disagreements between you, a tip that helps is to make sure you are reacting only to the current situation in front of you, and not to your internal world of memory and imagination. You will maintain your self-esteem if you stay, for example, a good brother, no matter what your brother or sister does, or stay a good mother or father, whatever your child does, or stay a good daughter or son, no matter what your parent does. Nothing I say here should be taken as implying you should stay in contact with an unambiguous abuser. Self-care is important, do not allow yourself to be abused.

When we have to deal with difficult people or situations, we will find it easier to stay reasonable if we consider what the present situation would look like from *outside*. What I mean by outside is: what would an objective observer, one who does not know about any past events between you and the person you are interacting with, and also no knowledge of the thoughts or feelings of either of you, say about your behaviour? What would they see if they were watching you on a video recording or through a window right now? The answer to that question can guide your actions by taking mind movies out of the equation and keeping you reacting to what is happening right here and right now.

A thorny relationship or one's uncomfortable feelings about a difficult person will not change quickly. Breaking down habitual emotional reactions takes time, and things between you may stay permanently difficult, particularly if the other person continues to react to past or imagined situations and events, and not to you as you are acting now. Generally speaking, however, if we can transform the way we treat someone in the now, over time our relationship with them will improve, as changes in us lead to changes in the other person, even if only small ones. Just remember though that how much a relationship can improve is not in your sole control. Sometimes, the value of tolerance and a goal to stay civil is enough. Be proud of your efforts.

TAKE ONE DAY AT A TIME

In the 1980s when I was in high school, the soap opera *Days of Our Lives* ran on early afternoon television. Some people liked to watch it as a time-out. The opening contained a voiceover that included the following statement, "Like sands through the hourglass, so are the days of our lives." Sands through the hourglass is an apt if unoriginal metaphor for the passage of time. The grains of sand in the top chamber of the hourglass are the future, the days yet to come. Day by day days enter into the narrow central waist of the glass. This narrow point represents the present, the now, the current instant or day. Each grain of sand has its moment passing through the centre, and then it falls into the bottom chamber. The grains of sand in the bottom chamber of the hourglass represent the days that have transited the narrow point of now and so are forever in the past.

Learning to think about the future and remember the past without getting emotionally entangled in them, can be imagined as learning to live in the centre of the hourglass, in the now. Our emotional brains, like those of other animals, are made to cope with the short-lived problems and challenges of *now*. But if we hold the grains as they fall and don't let the past go, if we try to force the future through that gap 'to process it now' or 'be ready for anything', we become stressed and cease to function. Our emotional responses were not designed to cope with the simultaneous onslaught of now, was, and will be, let alone hold steady if *might have been but wasn't* and *might be but isn't likely to be* are recruited into the battle against us. If everything is forced into the narrow point of now, and it goes on long enough, we may crack.

So if you have been struggling emotionally, take heart, don't be dismayed. It isn't likely that you can't cope if you take life moment by moment. Generally, when we are overwhelmed it is because we are trying to cope with too much time at once. As we discussed in Chapter 2: It's all about you, our emotions are not made for the extra burdens that come from imaginative entanglement in the past or the future, in other words, in the *not now*. The trouble is, that we humans with both imagination and language at our disposal, tend to spoil the now with worry about the future and with memories of past difficulties. Emotional responses to the *not now*, serve us not at all as responses to the *now*. Many people with vivid imaginations find planning how to handle every potential future misfortune, or remembering past problems and traumas, brings with it a flood of unpleasant emotions, for example, depression regarding what has happened, and anxiety about what is to come. It is necessary to recognise and accept our emotional responses as they happen because our current emotional state is part of now, and then it helps to remind oneself that whatever the event that a memory or worry is about, is not part of the now. The past is over. The future is yet to come.

To quote Paul Dubois:

> We poison the present by these apprehensions no less than
> by the useless memory of past misfortunes.

Another metaphor that makes the same point is the idea of standing on a bridge, under which run the rushing waters of time. The present time is the water now flowing under the bridge. If we bring forward water, hurrying it down from the mountains before its time, or hold the water under the bridge refusing to let it flow on, the water level under the bridge will rise, and we and the bridge will be inundated and at risk of being swept away. "That's all water under the bridge," and, "We'll cross that bridge when we come to it," are two expressions of the river under the bridge metaphor for time. They contain human wisdom accumulated over millennia. Which once again goes to show that nothing I am writing here is new.

While not suggesting you should always act on them, if you keep your attention focused in the now, your emotional responses will be appropriate to the now, or more correctly they will be the emotions our inner lizard and sheep think are appropriate!

EXPECT FUTURE PROBLEMS BUT DON'T OVER PREPARE

Trying to avoid stress by anticipating and preparing for every eventuality or by conducting detailed and repeated post-mortems of past troubles, rehearsing what we wished we had done is generally useless.

Many people have been told, and come to believe, that they must deeply process past traumas to heal from them, and that until this processing is done they cannot successfully move on. It is as if deconstructing the past, picking it apart and examining it, bone and sinew, could make a person immune from future ill fortune. It cannot and so it will not. Neither do you need to live out every possible scenario that the future may bring, in order to cope better with it, if and when it does occur. Not if you have the values of courage and kindness, etc., ready to guide you. A little planning is indeed useful, though it pays to remember that no one can avoid all misfortune. No matter how much you worry about the future, you will never predict or be able to make specific plans for every possible future problem. You might spend years worrying about a heart attack only to be run over by a bus. You might worry about an earthquake bringing down a building, but find your country attacked by a hostile force. The only thing sure about the future is that difficulties will arise. In the same way, no matter how long you ruminate over mistakes made or difficulties experienced in the past, no analysis of the specific cause of what went wrong, or what you might have done differently can make you immune to future problems. Pain and loss come to all.

What we need instead are values to live by, ones we know apply in every future situation and will ensure we cope well. Knowing that whatever comes you will face it with, for example, courage and kindness, means you can give up worrying and specific planning and instead face the future with confidence, reassured that whatever the future may unveil you will face it courageously and that you will face it kindly. Human trials are not unique. Many are the others who have faced grief, illness, imprisonment, loss of property and betrayal, and through it all inspired others with their courage, compassion and strength. So can you.

Stand on the bridge and watch the water flow, for the truth is that whatever will be will be.

RECOVER FROM TRAUMA AND LOSS

Dealing with past trauma and recovering from loss can be one of life's greatest challenges.

The past cannot be changed. That is the most important thing to accept. What is, *is*. It can be no other way. There is no enemy here to fight. The past is not a problem. It is a condition.

William James said in his 1897 work *The Will to Believe and Other Essays in Popular Philosophy*:

> Be willing to have it so. Acceptance of what has happened
> is the first step in overcoming any misfortune.

You are not unique in suffering. Pain is universal in human life. Believing mind stories about the uniqueness of our particular misfortune makes our suffering worse.

So what to do? The first thing is to let go of any guilt you hold for allowing the trauma to happen to you. For not fighting back, for not seeing the signs, for being in the wrong place at the wrong time, for not getting help earlier, etc. Remember whatever ideas your mind comes up with are part of its mission to identify any small areas where you can do something differently in the future, in order to avoid a similar event happening again. Identifying that there were small ways that you could have prevented it and potentially might prevent a similar event happening in the future does not mean what happened is your fault, not at all, and neither will such identifications prevent all future pain.

Don't feel guilty if your subconscious made you flop and drop so you were paralysed with fear and could not fight back (to be reminded about the flop and drop response see 'Fear and anxiety' in Chapter 4). Do as the Cynic philosophers and Stoics advise: only take responsibility for actions under your voluntary control. Do not be embarrassed about what you did not choose. The continuous you cannot be damaged by the actions of others. Shame rightfully belongs to the perpetrator of a crime, not to the victim. No one can take your dignity without your consent. For a reminder of the meaning of *the continuous you* see Chapter 2.

Again to quote Paul Dubois:

> It is pride, and the most vulgar sort, that makes us suffer when we have been deceived. We should then experience only one sorrow, that of having seen another go morally astray and show a low sentiment.

When you think about a past traumatic event or a loss that causes you grief, notice the feelings, notice the thoughts, notice the sadness, notice the pain with compassion and love. The hurting place inside you is not a threat. It needs love, not rejection. Hold uncomfortable thoughts as you would hold a crying baby. These are human thoughts: a marvel of the universe. Do not reject them. Notice also that the memories of loved ones that we have lost are precious as well as painful. They are like jewels on a crown of thorns.

When talking with a therapist or a friend about the really bad stuff that has happened to you in the past, you may have noticed it is not as upsetting to your inner lizard/sheep as when you remember it on your own. This is because in the presence of someone real, someone supportive, the mind is forced to notice reality, forced to acknowledge what is *here and now*. A therapy appointment is generally a safe place with someone who cares, so the mind movie of a traumatic memory is a little greyed out, and our emotional core is a little less upset. To put it another way, in the presence of another person there is an automatic expansion of aware-ness that brings a person back to the here and now, and in so doing lessens the intensity of the emotional response, most commonly fear, to the *not now*.

Practical advice for dealing with loss

1. Remember the past cannot be changed, "It is so, it cannot be otherwise."
2. Put a stop-loss order on mistakes
3. Cooperate with the inevitable
4. Keep busy
5. Don't fuss about little things

6. Remember the law of averages: "You win some you lose some."

There's a big difference between acceptance of what is, and what is includes whatever one is feeling now, and acceptance as the end stage of the grieving process as popularised in the work of Elizabeth Kubler-Ross (Kessler and Kubler-Ross, 2005). In Ross's model, a grieving individual moves back and forth, and finally through five stages of grief. The five stages are denial, anger, bargaining, depression and acceptance. I do not doubt the value of this work, but acceptance as referred to in ACT and in this book, is acceptance for the now. It is acceptance of sadness, guilt, anger and denial and maybe in time acceptance of acceptance as well. It is not a stage to aim for, not a time at which we will no longer feel sad, guilty or angry. It is not a future stage that when achieved will eliminate one's pain. In ACT and in this book acceptance means accepting yourself and your feelings as they are now, and in their presence to find a way to live towards one's values.

ANGER, HATRED AND REVENGE

Anger quickly becomes irrational, even when it's justified. And anger creates anger in our adversary, anger that could, as stated in Proverbs 15:1, be turned aside by a gentle word. Anger is a challenging emotion because, like the fear response, it bypasses the slower reasoning parts of our minds. When we are angry, we become unable to think, unable to process information, to learn or even to form

memories. If, however, we can avoid getting angry, by practising as much tolerance and forgiveness as we muster, we
may have enough energy and mental capacity to do something constructive about a difficult situation.

More from Seneca, who had rather a lot to say on anger.
Maybe it came from trying to advise Nero!

The eager and self-destructive violence of anger does not
grow up by slow degrees, but reaches its full height as soon
as it begins. Nor does it, like other vices, merely disturb
men's minds, but it takes them away, and torments them
till they are incapable of restraining themselves and eager
for the common ruin of all men, nor does it rage merely
against its object, but against every obstacle which it
encounters on its way. ... Other vices affect our judgment,
anger affects our sanity: others come in mild attacks and
grow unnoticed, but men's minds plunge abruptly into
anger. ... Its intensity is in no way regulated by its origin: for
it rises to the greatest heights from the most trivial
beginnings.

We shall succeed in avoiding anger, if from time to time we
lay before our minds all the vices connected with anger,
and estimate it at its real value: it must be prosecuted
before us and convicted: its evils must be thoroughly inves-
tigated and exposed.

...anger pays a penalty at the same moment that it exacts
one: it forswears human feelings. The latter urge us to love,
anger urges us to hatred: the latter bid us do men good,

anger bids us do them harm. ... How far more glorious is it to throw back all wrongs and insults from oneself, like one wearing armour... proof against all weapons, for revenge is an admission that we have been hurt.

The difference between planned and unplanned actions, for example, between acts of violence committed under the influence of violent emotion, and acts of violence committed *in cold blood* is, in many nations, recognised in law. Such a distinction is, for example, the rationale for distinguishing between different degrees of murder. First-degree murder involves a premeditated plan to kill. The neocortex is a criminal in first-degree murder. It is not an act of passion, not just of emotion, committed during a momentary loss of self-control, but instead involves a corruption of thought. Second-degree murder involves no such plan. While unpractised reason, perhaps weakened by alcohol, stood by and did not exert appropriate restraint, reason was not *a part of it all along*. Religion too recognises this difference. Crimes of passion are seen as more excusable than those resulting from the perversion of human reason. Crimes of a cold, clinical and premeditated kind are therefore regarded as more immoral. Remember that revenge is always such a crime. It is always planned; it always involves thought. It is different from simple retaliation. In Dante's *Inferno*, the outer circles of hell house those who give way to animal passions, and these are less tormenting than the inner circles, wherein those who abused human reason to abet their evil, for example, fraudsters and traitors are condemned to suffer. Dante's imagined placement of the circles largely aligns with earlier classifications of vice, such as that found in Aristotle's *Ethics* dating from the 4th Century BC.

Most people get angry from time to time, with their partners, their children, with other drivers or even random passersby, but we don't generally hate the objects of our temporary anger. A few minutes after your anger has abated, your feelings about the person you were angry with, are likely to be pretty much the same as before you got angry. You love them if they are a family member, or feel pretty well indifferent towards them if they were a stranger on the street. It's only when, and if, you specifically remember the event that provoked your anger that the memory may stir up your anger again.

Expressing anger tends to increase it, not diminish it. Instead of taking revenge and calling it justice, or making pointless complaints, seek justice by finding a way to prevent the same or a similar harm from being perpetrated on another person. And, what is probably the most important, can you forgive yourself for feeling anger at all? Please forgive yourself for feeling anger with or the desire for revenge against those who have hurt you. These are after all, not feelings you chose to have!

Hatred is not so specific. It's not about a particular event, place or time, instead it spreads and eats up even good things you remember about a person or group of people. Hatred becomes about the person or group of people themselves and no longer about specific times or specific actions. The thought of *them*, not any particular event, causes anger.

Anger can burst from where it smoulders in memory into a sudden inferno. Hate can tempt a person to indulge in revenge fantasies even if one is committed to non-violence.

Hatred is usually the result of repeated experiences of abuse. Many people have never hated anyone in this way, and that is a good thing. But, if, what you have experienced, or seen experienced by a loved one, has been so traumatic that the very mention of a name causes burning anger and a flood of adrenalin through your body, then that is hatred. It is an uncomfortable but all too natural feeling.

To deal with hatred, a useful first step is to be glad you were the victim and not the perpetrator. How much worse would it be to be the one who did the evil deeds that have earned your hatred? How terrible to be so ignorant or so morally corrupt as they must be to have acted in this way? And how terrible to be hated the way they are hated by you? Can you feel sorry for them instead? Then secondly remember that you have survived, you're alive and though you may feel as damaged as a charred stick, you are still you, you are not a pile of ashes. Jesus suggested his followers pray for their enemies (Luke 6:27-28 New International Version). Can you keep in mind that they too are victims?

> But to you who are listening I say: Love your enemies, do good to those who hate you, bless those who curse you, pray for those who mistreat you.

Remember you are not in charge of your emotions, only your actions and that depending on the extent of the injustice or harm done or being done to you or those you love, you may have to accept, at least for a time, the shadows of incompletely eliminated hate within yourself as you choose to act with love instead.

A quote from Seneca, Stoic teacher of the first century AD:

> Revenge takes up much time, and throws itself in the way of many injuries while it is smarting under one. We all retain our anger longer than we feel our hurt. ... Would anyone think himself to be in his perfect mind if he were to return kicks to a mule or bites to a dog? ... If animals are protected from your anger by their want of reason, you ought to treat all foolish men in the like manner.

THOUGHTS ON BLAME

Blame seems to be able to add up to much more than 100% as we try to distribute it in terms of how likely it is, that we, or someone else, could have prevented any particular event, if we had taken a different action or actions from the ones we actually took.

> If only I hadn't gone to the shops that day ...
> If only he'd called me a day or two earlier ...
> If only the shop assistant had served me a bit more quickly ...
> If only I had gone home directly ...

and on and on ...

Just about anyone can be blamed, for almost anything, given the way the consequences of our actions spread like ripples. No wonder scapegoating is so popular, and so also its opposite, which is taking all the blame onto oneself.

If we try to apportion blame, what do we come up with? "It's 80% her fault, 90% his fault, 90% their fault and all my fault!"

Until you come back to the final point, where the buck stops and that's with the guy at the top. It's God's fault. God is to blame for what happened, for isn't he in charge of everything, everything preordained? Or if he's not directly to blame, then he is to blame indirectly, for making a world in which this could happen! Yes, people do think like this and it can cause them to lose their faith. But what sense is there in blaming God?

When potentially avoidable misfortune strikes in the form of a car accident, a suicide, a divorce, an act of violence, a workplace injury, a descent into drug or gambling addiction, an unwanted pregnancy, a lost pet, a house fire, a plane crash, a medication error, a robbery ... you name it, there are so many misfortunes available to choose from, I suggest you consider that there is no single reason for it happening, and no one person entirely to blame. In nearly all cases, there existed multiple points at which the event could have been prevented, if someone, or anyone, had acted differently!

The truth is that a lot of things have to come together for anything momentous to happen, the stars have to align as it were. The ancients recognised this, and so the conjunction of heavenly bodies was seen as a sign of consequential events about to take place.

The difference between a miss, a near-miss, and plain sailing, is only in the alignment of small gaps. It is when all the holes line up right through the cheese that an unfortunate event happens, as if one could fall through a block of Swiss cheese if all the holes aligned. In this Swiss cheese analogy, each small personal failing and random event in the long overlapping chain of reasons that lead up to an unfortunate event are the small air holes.

Random events can never be explained. Why did a car happen to be coming down the usually quiet street at the same moment a child's ball rolled onto the road? And then there are the numerous small human failings involving many individual people. Why didn't you close the gate? Why weren't you standing closer? Why was he driving so fast?

If any hole had not been there, or if it had been in a different place, then whatever happened would not have happened. So, there is not one reason but many, and many, many places and many people, on which the blame for any tragedy may be laid.

We cannot move through the cheese, beyond our place in time and space to see where all the holes are, or where they will ever form. And even if we did see all the holes, much of the blame would still have to be put down to sheer bad luck and random chance. We need to accept we humans simply cannot know all the reasons why anything that happens, happens.

We can be a hole in a chain leading up to tragedy so early that we never know we contributed to it, but when we do see we have been close to the end of such a chain of failings that ended in disaster, pain or loss, we tend to blame ourselves, or those just behind or in front of us in the line of holes. The mind may flip back and forth between its desire for power, and its desire to avoid guilt as it tries and fails to find a way to be both blameless and in control. Our emotions and thoughts are in turmoil, for if it is true we had the power of prevention, we are to blame and so we feel guilt. But if we will not accept any guilt, it means we were powerless to prevent the tragedy, and if we were powerless, we are vulnerable to such an event happening again, and so we feel fear. The mind wants what it can't have, and so it cannot rest.

The truth is between. We and many others share a little guilt and share a little power too.

When we understand that all our actions form either safety, or form risk, for ourselves and others, that every kindness, however small, matters, that a single smile at a stranger can prevent a tragedy, or that an angry frown at someone under stress can form an air bubble, a gap in their already hole-ridden safety net, we can understand the importance of always being kind, always being just and always being forgiving.

REFLECT ON YOUR ACTIONS DAILY

Remember every day is a precious gift, and it like a gift of fresh flowers will not last. Time is transient, each moment ephemeral, like a drop of rain falling. There is no saving time in a bottle. All we can do is take care of this day, take care of its constituent moments, so that tonight as the light fades and night unfolds, we can reflect with happiness on the beautiful day we created.

Once you decide to set your sights on living your values, to place virtue above all other goals, you will find it good practice to do an evening reflection on your day. During your reflection, focus on decisions you made and actions you took that had moral relevance. How did you manage irritation? Did you give way to anger? What bad habits did you follow? What vice did you refrain from? Write a couple of lines summarizing how well you lived your values. Your answers will reveal what sort of actions lead to you feeling pleased with yourself at the end of the day, and which do not. It is important to give yourself some positive feedback and encouragement in recognition of the efforts you are making. Nightly reflection isn't meant to be a session of self-abuse. All teachers know that feedback should not be entirely negative. Remember your evening reflection is a form of self-instruction.

From Seneca's essay on anger:

> Anger will cease and become more gentle if it knows that every day it will have to appear before the judgement seat.
>
> I pardon you this time, see that you never do that anymore.

Where thoughts or feelings led you off course, see if you can identify what happened, why it happened, and what support or encouragement you might give yourself next time. Having made an honest assessment, forgive yourself and resolve to do better. Be your own friend and coach. Say, "Today was a good day. I used time wisely. I was kind to... I could have done better when... What I have learnt is..., etc." Remember the task isn't easy and your job during your reflection is to encourage your efforts and persistence. Many things sound simple, but take a lot of effort and determination, and that includes living by values. Every day comes with challenges, and when they do not throw you off course, celebrate. When they do, don't be alarmed, just look at what happened, forgive and try again tomorrow.

A morning reflection is also useful. Every day is a new slice of time that has never been before, innocent and perfect, untainted by any past event. Is there a particular value you want to live today? One that you will particularly need given anticipated challenges? Even if none are expected, they can still happen so be prepared.

The advice Marcus Aurelius gave to himself may be helpful:

When you wake up in the morning, tell yourself: the people I deal with today will be meddling, ungrateful, arrogant, dishonest, jealous and surly. They are like this because they can't tell good from evil. But I have seen the beauty of good, and the ugliness of evil, and have recognized that the wrongdoer has a nature related to my own − not of the same blood and birth, but the same mind, and possessing a share of the divine. And so none of them can hurt me. No one can implicate me in ugliness. Nor can I feel angry at my relative, or hate him. We were born to work together like feet, hands and eyes, like the two rows of teeth, upper and lower. To obstruct each other is unnatural. To feel anger at someone, to turn your back on him: these are unnatural.

Values are like tools in a toolkit we carry each day on our life journey. Patience is a tool we need nearly every day, so take patience with you everywhere and use it whenever needed. What else will you pack in your toolkit today?

spiritual help for living – how faith can help you be happy

WHY IT HELPS TO BELIEVE

You don't need to believe in the God of the three Abrahamic faiths (Judaism, Islam and Christianity) or any other personal god to access spiritual help in living out your values and reaching your goals. Access to spiritual resources only requires you to believe in something greater than yourself. It can be a personal god or a spiritual concept for example *the divine*. You may ask: What defines a personal God and distinguishes them from a more amorphous concept like *the divine*? Simply put, a personal God is a *person*, that is, a being who has a history, who can make choices and take actions, while a concept, say God defined as divine unchanging good, does not make choices and does not take actions. The traditional God of the Abrahamic faiths is a person, he makes choices and takes actions, for example, the choice to create the world, or the choice to give humans free will. Both imaginings of God can provide spiritual inspiration and support to a human quest to live out one's values. But believing God is a person provides an extra motivating force which supports religious people in living towards values and creating second happiness, because not only do they want to please themselves and make themselves happy, they want to please God too. A personal God can have relationships, a personal God can be pleased. A concept cannot.

If one accepts a personal God, it doesn't mean one has to believe he actively intervenes in the created world. A personal God can mostly let the physical world run entirely in accord with physical and material laws. It doesn't mean you have to start believing in miracles or being a biblical literalist.

Because the nature of God is good (wisdom, justice, good-ness, truth, mercy, love and so on) wanting to please God means wanting to live by moral values. This is particularly valuable when the idea of living doing good and living in accordance with *my* values to make *me* happy doesn't seem like it's worth much as may be the case for a person whose self-esteem is at rock bottom. "Why does it matter what I think is important? Why should I be happy anyway? I am a rotten person, with rotten thoughts, etc."

Self-chosen values can only effectively motivate behavioural change in the setting of at least a little bit of self-love. Without any self-love at all, when self-esteem is virtually non-existent, a person can be reduced to feeling that every breath they take is a waste of oxygen. In such cases living to please God becomes the necessary fuel to drive movement towards values, and so to the recovery of self-esteem. Once self-esteem begins to return, a person can once again see themselves as someone whose values and whose ultimate happiness matters. Nothing can grow without a seed, and wanting to please God can be that seed.

As well as providing a seed from which recovery of one's sense of value can grow, religious faith also gives meaning to perseverance through hardship. So it is worth making an effort to hold a sense of worship to God within yourself while you do things you find difficult. Even a non-personal concept of *the divine* can be effective in this regard. Difficult things are easier to do if they are not for nothing, not for nobody, not if your words and actions are an offering of love.

Viktor Frankl was a young Jewish doctor at the outbreak of the Second World War. He survived internment in three separate concentration camps. In his memoir *Man's Search for Meaning* he said:

> Life is never made unbearable by circumstances, but only by lack of meaning and purpose.

> In some ways suffering ceases to be suffering at the moment it finds a meaning, for example, the meaning of a sacrifice.

The French-Swiss neuropathologist and psychotherapist, Paul Dubois, talked about the assistance of spiritual ideas to guide our search for fulfilment.

In his influential early 20th century work *Self-control and How to Secure it* he said:

> ... a religion of spirit, a continual effort to live well, has immense force...
>
> I have tried to show how altruistic feelings are created by rational mental representations and lead us to find a guide in a moral idea. That is the efficacious spiritualism we need; to avoid all confusion, I will call it idealism. It matters little that our opinions differ upon insoluble subjects of metaphysic, that we explain by dualistic or monistic theories phenomena whose essence escape us; the important thing is to seek happiness in the realization of our ideal.

Some critics of religion say it is a crutch for those too weak to walk unsupported. It seems odd to me that the same people who say religion is a crutch, are often the most determined to destroy the faith of others. Isn't that like going around taking away the crutches of cripples, or the walking frames of the elderly? Why would you do that? And anyway aren't we all weak? Aren't we all human? We can all use a walking pole or even two poles, when the track gets rough, and a camel swimming in deep water, even one with water wings, could sure use a lifejacket or, even better, a boat at times! So, take the help your traditions offer you. Don't be too proud.

Judeo-Christian tradition pervades this book for that is my heritage. In its centuries of accumulated wisdom, in its contemplations and central teachings is treasure. But, many religions make seaworthy vessels capable of taking their followers safely across the sea of life. The best one for you is usually the one you were born into, in terms of your family or wider cultural heritage because coming to a full understanding of a religion is as difficult as learning to understand a language.

Affirmation and approval of emotion is an essential part of Christianity, Islam and Judaism sourced both from the conviction that all God creates, including human feelings, is good and from scriptural descriptions of God's emotions, in particular his love for his creation. Understanding our emotions as good, promotes respect for human love, for example, the love that binds families. In Christianity there is no shame in feeling family love or natural emotional pain. Jesus wept on hearing of the death of his friend Lazarus (John 11:35), and while on the cross he showed concern for his mother, entrusting her to the care of one of his closest friends (John 19:26-27).

All systems of faith are built upon a set of foundational beliefs. Foundational beliefs are the things accepted as *givens*. They require no justification. Foundational beliefs that support a rational religion, must however not contradict each other, and none should have been proven false. Christian and Jewish thinkers involved in critical enquiry down the centuries, starting perhaps with Moses and ending with Karl Barth, George Lindbeck and others, have identified several foundational beliefs which ground Judaism and so also its offshoot Christianity. Four foundational beliefs important to me are:

There is only one God.

God is the only Creator.

God is Good.

God wants to be in relationship with us and his world.

From these foundations it follows that earth is good as is every other component of the universe. There is no second divine entity who creates evil and evil creatures as postulated in Zoroastrianism. It means that the oceans, the waterfalls, the sunbeams, the sparrows, the corn, the eels, the ducks, all that exists is part of an ongoing creation with a time to be and a purpose. Thus, the physical world is not an illusion, it is not a prison for souls as Platonists or Gnostics suggested, we have not fallen by accident into bodies. The Earth and not heaven is the place humans were created in and for.

1 Timothy 4:4. New Living Translation:

> Since everything God created is good, we should not reject any of it but receive it with thanks.

Some people think that wasps and mosquitoes have no purpose. If they would expand their view a little, they would see that mosquito larvae feed fish and adult mosquitoes feed frogs, and welcome swallows too. Wasps too are needed for they prey on insects and spiders and keep the natural balance, so preventing the decimation of food crops by plagues of caterpillars. So do sparrows and other birds, which feed their young with insects. Regarding sparrows as pests and encouraging their systematic killing allowed swarms of locusts to decimate rice fields and led to severe famine in China with at least 20 million human deaths from starvation between 1958 and 1962 (Kreston, 2014).

Faith is a choice to believe what you do not know beyond reasonable doubt. Doubt is therefore part of the very definition of faith. Faith is not knowledge, it is about relationship, it is about trust. For example, if you tell me that you have done something, I can choose to trust that you are telling me the truth. On the other hand, if I *knew*, if, for example, I had seen you do it, I would have *knowledge*, not faith. Thus the very *essence* of faith is in not being able to offer proof. It is, however, essential, to any rational form of faith, that it lets go of beliefs that have been proven false, for example, belief in a flat earth. I believe that biblical interpretations, like all other human creations, should be examined in the light of human reason, and pass helpfulness and humanity checks!

The Bible is not a single book, it is a collection of books. It holds many voices, not just one voice. It was not written all at once, and it is not just one genre. Nor does it present just one philosophical view of metaphysics (the ultimate nature of reality). Critics of the Judeo-Christian tradition hold these scriptural fissures and contradictions up as faults. I hold them up as the expansion gaps on railway tracks that stop them warping in hot weather and derailing trains, or the seismic joints in a building that let it move and so stop earthquakes bringing it down. It is quite certain I could not stay inside the tent of Christianity, without its ability to bend and stretch and hold me tight, just as if I were a fish in a fishing net. Jesus is recorded in Matthew 4:19 (New International Version) as saying:

> "Come, follow me," Jesus said, "and I will send you out to fish for people."

WHY DOES SUFFERING EXIST IF GOD IS GOOD?

Some questions are like a puzzle made from a set of square tiles on which an artist first drew a picture on one side, then after turning all the tiles over, rearranged them and drew another picture on the second side. In such a scenario, it is impossible to put both pictures together at once. There is simply no way to assemble the pieces so that two people looking at the puzzle from opposite sides can at once agree that the placement of the tiles is correct. The more you put the picture on one side together, the more the picture on the other side gets broken.

Suffering in the world is a difficult question for adherents of monotheistic religions which claim that God is at once all-powerful and all-good. We cannot easily explain evil as the creation of an evil god acting in opposition to the true God as some faiths do. The three Abrahamic monotheistic faith traditions, Judaism, Christianity and Islam, share the belief that even Satan himself was created good, being at one time a holy and powerful angel. So why do people suffer? Why is there evil in the world? This profound question even has its own name: theodicy, and over the centuries there have been many answers.

Some answers I have heard offered do not seem at all convincing, for example, that all the suffering we see is due to choices made by Adam and Eve in a literal Garden of Eden, and that before those two sinned the world was perfect. Or that every individual event of suffering is a part of God's huge grand design, and that the beauty of this plan requires that certain threads and lives be cut short for the beauty of the whole. This idea may make a certain kind of sense, but seems to contradict the immense value of individual people, which is after all a concept central to Christian teaching, as seen in the parables of "The Lost Sheep", "The Lost Coin" and "The Prodigal Son" recorded in the Gospel of Luke. Christianity teaches that trees as well as forests matter, and that the world is to be saved not by utopian movements but by individual acts of love.

Others see suffering on earth as punishment for individual sin. But again this contradicts the teaching of Jesus himself. There is a story in chapter 9 of the Gospel of John about Jesus giving sight to a man who had been blind since birth. Jesus's disciples assume the man's blindness is a punishment for sin, and are therefore confused by his having been born blind. Note that in Judaism, there is no concept of reincarnation to conveniently explain away afflictions suffered by innocent children and infants as fair punishments for infractions in past lives. Jesus tells his followers that human afflictions are not punishments for sin but opportunities for love (John 9:1-3. New King James Version):

> Now as Jesus passed by, He saw a man who was blind from birth. And His disciples asked Him, saying, "Rabbi, who sinned, this man or his parents, that he was born blind?"
>
> Jesus answered, "Neither this man nor his parents sinned, but that the works of God should be revealed in him."

I have come to believe, as have many Christian thinkers over the centuries, that suffering exists because God's ultimate aim is the creation of kindness. He made us in his image, with the freedom to choose both good and evil because without the freedom to do evil and cause pain to ourselves and to others, we cannot choose love or moral good. There can be no altruism, no compassion, no love, in a clockwork pain-free world and that is why we have the world we do.

WAR AND RELIGION

Many contend that religion causes wars, and use this to argue that humans should abandon religion and spiritual concepts entirely. They are not wrong in their belief that religion can cause war, it can. Many human ideas, potentially even the idea that religion causes war, could lead to war if we decide to fight about it and rally others to join us! But before we stop believing, remember that religious ideas can and do stop wars too. Ideas are things of the neocortex, of the imagination, they can work up natural aggression in the more primitive parts of our brains or damp it down.

Conflict, and even war, is everywhere in the animal world. It is not a uniquely human phenomenon. Male seals fight bloody battles to monopolise a patch of sand and the females occupying it. Gorillas and chimpanzees raid their neighbours and even sometimes kill the young of rival troops. Ant colonies wage war and even take slaves. It is in our animal nature that the base causes of war and violence lie, in greed, envy, selfishness and the drive for dominance.

Again, I agree with the critics of religion, that religion can whip up aggression. Look at ideas of God-given land possession in the Middle East that grip both sides of that enduring conflict. So yes, ideas can cause wars, not just religious ideas, non-religious political or other ideological systems, can and do as well. Ideas can make people do evil things, or do good things. So, saying, "Religion causes war," means nothing more than saying, "Ideas cause war."

What can take us forward from such an inane and obvious assertion, is the determination that our religions should be based on good ideas, not bad ones. Good ideas about justice, tolerance, love, peace, equality, the one-familyness of all, the value and goodness of the natural world and so on. If religions teach these things, they will promote peace, not war. But if a religion teaches racial superiority, animal or human sacrifice, sexism, conformity, unthinking submission to authority and so on, it may promote injustice, violence and war. Bad religious ideas that fail helpfulness and humanity tests are ideas best abandoned.

If you agree with me that religious ideas and scriptural interpretations need to pass a compassion or humanity test, you may be interested in the work of Charterforcompassion.org which supports the Charter for Compassion (Armstrong 2011). The charter advocates that all religious ideas and interpretations of scripture be subjected to a litmus test of compassion.

Good religions (by which I mean those defined by adherence to the primacy of compassion), also function as guard rails restraining state tyranny by teaching that governments and monarchs have to answer to a higher moral authority (i.e. that they too are subjects of God). The inhumanity of Nazi Germany, the millions of Russians and others who died while power was in the hands of atheist dictator Stalin (who desired to stamp out religion from Russia) and the millions of Cambodian deaths under the Pol Pot regimen (which had as one of its stated aims the elimination of Cambodian Buddhism) are well-known examples of government actions unfettered by moral restraint.

CHRISTIAN FORGIVENESS

Jesus asked his followers to extend radical forgiveness to those who do them wrong. The following conversation, between Peter and Jesus, is recorded in the Gospel of Matthew (Matthew 18:21-22. New International Version):

> Then Peter came to Jesus and asked, "Lord, how many times shall I forgive my brother or sister who sins against me? Up to seven times?" Jesus answered, "I tell you, not seven times, but seventy-seven times."

Let's start by looking at what Christian forgiveness is.

New Testament teaching on forgiveness links instructions not to judge others with the instruction to aim at the highest of moral virtue. Jesus is recorded as having said the following (Matthew 5:43-48. New International Version):

> You have heard that it was said, "Love your neighbour and hate your enemy" But I tell you, love your enemies and pray for those who persecute you, that you may be children of your Father in heaven. He causes his sun to rise on the evil and the good, and sends rain on the righteous and the unrighteous. If you love those who love you, what reward will you get? Are not even the tax collectors doing that? And if you greet only your own people, what are you doing more than others? Do not even pagans do that? Be perfect, there-fore, as your heavenly Father is perfect.

Jesus said we are to aim at perfection. This means that though our lives and actions will inevitably fall far short of the target, we are to be like arrows shot at the moon. This is my first point about what forgiveness is. Forgiveness is not a compromise of morality.

Loving others and ourselves means we should never allow evil we can prevent from continuing. This is my second point about forgiveness. It does not mean tolerating abuse or evil.

What about justice? If we forgive hurts done to us, does that violate justice? No. Christian forgiveness means leaving the fulfilment of justice to the one best fitted to that task, the

God who sees into the hearts of everyone, who knows the motives and circumstances of all events. We are not God; we do not know all the reasons of our own hearts, let alone anyone else's. We do not know what justice is.

So, now we know what forgiveness is not, what is it that Jesus asks us to do?

Human forgiveness means releasing someone from having a personal debt to us. When we forgive a loan, it means we no longer require or expect a debtor to pay us back. Just as we can forgive a loan, we can forgive other people for both real and perceived harm done to us. This is what Jesus was telling his followers: that they should not hold anything against other people. They should not expect or attempt to exact personal reckoning or retribution, but instead release the debt and move on. Forgiveness means no longer requiring anything from the other person, no apology, no punishment, no admission of wrongdoing, nothing. It does not necessitate one forget an evil was done, or specify that we should continue in relationship with an abuser.

Prudence requires that we learn from what has been done. If it is right for us, if it is safe for us, then after forgiving, we can reconcile with a person who has done us wrong, accepting their and our imperfections and limitations. If it is not safe, then instead forgive from a distance. It is enough that we let go of the need for repayment and do not seek retribution or revenge. We do not need to feel a cosy, warm feeling towards them.

This is a point worth expanding: forgiveness can be done from a safe distance. Since we are not asking for remorse, apology or understanding, it does not need to involve the other person. You don't need to let someone know they are forgiven, and you can forgive someone who has died. It is we, and we alone, who release the debt. It is we who free ourselves.

So how do we forgive?

It can be difficult, but it helps to remember that the answer to why someone hurt you may well lie in their trauma and hurt, in past events we just can't know. Because of this, asking, "Why me?" "What did I do to deserve this?" "Why did he/she treat me this way?" and the like, whether it's a rude shop assistant or a distant and cold parent isn't the right question. Very likely it wasn't about you at all.

Second, we can acknowledge what we know is true: that we will have appeared unreasonable, or even deliberately unkind to others on many occasions. We need forgiveness too. None of us can make amends for every unkind or unjust action we have ever performed, whether in weakness, ignorance or by wilful choice. Our hope lies in God's and in other people's forgiveness of us, and in the forgiveness that Jesus asks us to give to others. Forgiving others is a response to our imperfect state. It is an act of humility.

Consider the following Scriptures (1 Corinthians 2:11. Living Bible):

No one can really know what anyone else is thinking or what he is really like...

Here is a reminder we have a limited understanding of others and their motives (Proverbs 24:29. Good News Translation):

Don't say "I'll do to them just what they did to me! I'll get even with them!"

A reminder we should not try to get even (Luke 23:34. New International Version):

Father forgive them; for they do not know what they are doing.

Words of Jesus spoken on the cross which remind us that abusers often lack an understanding of their own actions.

Radical forgiveness for deliberate evil does not come naturally to any of us, and when the hurt and harm done is deep, God's assistance is required. Knowing this, Jesus incorporated, into the prayer he composed and taught his followers, a request for assistance in forgiving and a reminder that none of us is innocent, but are all in need of forgiveness too (Matthew 6:12. New International Version):

And forgive us our debts, as we also have forgiven our debtors.

And Luke 11:4. New International Version:

Forgive us our sins, for we also forgive everyone who sins against us.

And finally, consider St Paul's words recorded in Romans 12:19. New International Version:

Do not take revenge, my dear friends, but leave room for God's wrath, for it is written: "It is mine to avenge; I will repay," says the Lord.

By referring to God's promise to punish wrong doing as recorded in Deuteronomy 32:35, St Paul reminds his readers in Rome, and us down the centuries, that final justice is in the hands of the one impartial and all-knowing judge.

Everyday forgiveness for minor offences is also important, for all of us have been hurt at times by the actions of others. Sometimes offence is intentional, but more often it is not. It is instead, the result of ignorance, misunderstanding or carelessness. Minor offences, unintended and intended, are inevitable in our everyday lives, as we interact with other imperfect people. The teaching of Jesus on how to respond to minor offences is, just like his teaching regarding forgiveness for more serious evil-doing, very clear.

Matthew 5:39. New International Version:

...If anyone slaps you on the right cheek, turn to them the other cheek also.

In biblical times, as now, the metaphor "a slap in the face" was used to describe an unexpected insult or offence. What Jesus is saying is that if someone insults you, don't react with anger. Don't get upset and return insult for insult. Let someone insult you again if they want to. Turn the other cheek.

In his discussion of this verse in his 1708 commentary, British Nonconformist minister and author, Matthew Henry wrote:

> Suffer any injury that can be borne, for the sake of peace, committing your concerns to the Lord's keeping. And the sum of all is, that Christians must avoid disputing and striving. If any say, Flesh and blood cannot pass by such an affront, let them remember, that flesh and blood shall not inherit the kingdom of God; and those who act upon right principles will have the most peace and comfort.

In summary: forgiveness is not calling something somebody else did that was immoral or destructive, okay. Forgiveness means you choosing to release that somebody from personal obligation to you. It does not require a soft-hearted feeling towards the person who harmed you, but it does require you to hold back from revenge. It requires that you trust God with the responsibility of judgement and the dispensing of ultimate justice. It also means daily refraining from the need to defend our honour by engaging in petty and personal disputes.

SERENITY PRAYER THOUGHTS

"The Serenity Prayer" as we have come to know it, was written by German American theologian Reinhold Niebuhr who lived from 1892 to 1971, however, the sentiments conveyed have many earlier expressions dating back to Aristotle and perhaps beyond, leading to many discussions regarding the true origin of the prayer.

In writing a reflection on "The Serenity Prayer" to be used as part of a church service, I discovered something very interesting. The prayer covers nearly everything we have been discussing up to this point! Because of this, you will find in reading this section, repeats of material already covered, although here referenced to the prayer and so it makes a good concluding section to this book.

"The Serenity Prayer" talks about taking one day at a time, it talks about accepting things, it talks about finding joy in the present moment, it talks about recognising the reality of evil in the world, it talks about placing the pursuit of virtue above all else, it tells us that this is the way to be happy in this world, and it recognises even our best effort cannot eliminate natural pain. "The Serenity Prayer" is thus a synopsis of enduring psychological wisdom, something to be celebrated.

I imagine all of us have heard this prayer in its popular short form:

God, grant me the Serenity
To accept the things I cannot change...
Courage to change the things I can,
And Wisdom to know the difference.

Reinhold Niebuhr is reported to have first used the prayer as the final part of a longer prayer in around 1932.

The prayer has achieved a very wide distribution, spreading through the YWCA and other groups in the 1930s, and in Alcoholics Anonymous and related organisations since at least 1941. Today you can find it on fridge magnets, greeting cards, bookmarks, T-shirts, posters and more.

Pastor Niebuhr also wrote an expanded version of the prayer which makes plain several important points, that might easily be missed in the shorter version. It is this longer version, on which I would like to share some thoughts.

God, give us grace to accept with serenity
the things that cannot be changed,
Courage to change the things
which should be changed,
and the Wisdom to distinguish
the one from the other.
Living one day at a time,
Enjoying one moment at a time,
Accepting hardship as a pathway to peace,
Taking, as Jesus did,
This sinful world as it is,
Not as I would have it,

Trusting that You will make all things right,
If I surrender to Your will,
So that I may be reasonably happy in this life,
And supremely happy with You forever in the
    next.
Amen.

This longer prayer can be examined line by line. The first line reads, "God, give us grace to accept with serenity the things that cannot be changed". When we accept things that cannot be changed instead of fighting the inevitable, serenity results. The Stoic philosopher Epictetus taught that human life is like the life of a dog tied to the cart of fate by a long rope. Knowing it cannot stop the cart, the best thing for the dog to do is to get up and move, whenever and wherever the cart goes. The long rope will then provide the dog with some freedom. The only other option is to be dragged along by its neck. The point is, you don't have to like the way things are to accept them, and you will have more freedom and more happiness if you acknowledge the limits of your power. In other words, trying to resist the inevitable is the cause of much human distress.

Epictetus lived and taught from around 50 to 135 AD. He was born a slave in the city of Hierapolis, present-day Pamukkale, in western Turkey. He later taught in Rome and then in Nicopolis in northwestern Greece. Epictetus, like Jesus, was a teacher, not a writer, however, his teachings were written down and published by his pupil Arrian as, among other works, *The Discourses of Epictetus* and *The Handbook* or *Enchiridion*.

The second line reads, "Courage to change the things which should be changed". We all need courage to take the action or actions that we can take, which we know to be right. Courage to tell the truth, courage to take risks for others, courage to be ourselves and not fall in with whatever opinions or behaviours are in fashion. Courage to stand up for what we believe in, courage to risk rejection, isolation or punishment or if it should be necessary to bear these things.

The third line of the prayer asks God for the wisdom to distinguish the one from the other. The wisdom being asked for is the ability to look at the things we don't like and see that they fall into two groups, and therefore can be sorted into two baskets. They are either conditions we don't like but should be accepting, or they are problems which we don't like but can work towards changing. So, how do we tell conditions and problems apart?

The difference is simply that we cannot change a condition, while a problem can, with effort, be changed. For example, if we don't like getting wet, a broken zip on a raincoat is a problem we can change, while a wet day is a condition to be accepted. It is a question of what we have power over, what we can control that makes the difference between a problem and a condition. I believe this is the most important line of the prayer, to ask God for the wisdom to distinguish a condition from a problem. If we think we can change or control things that are out of our control, we will have many unsolvable problems and so misery will result.

So many things are out of our control: the passage of time, our past, who our parents were, the place we were born, the language we learnt as an infant, the actions of others, even including those whom we love the most. We aren't even in full control of our thoughts: the memories we have, or when they, or random and sometimes uncharitable thoughts may come to mind. We don't choose these. Our brains simply do not have a delete button in handy reach, that we can push so a thought or a memory we don't like never comes to mind again.

What are some examples of conditions that sometimes get mistaken for problems? Here are a few: we can't simply choose to like something or someone, again in contrast to our computers, we do not have a *sleep button* we can push and go to sleep at will, we cannot change the past or forget a hurt or injustice done to us, we can't love someone just because we think we should, and we can't be someone of a different race, or be taller, shorter or with different sex chromosomes than those we have. All these things are therefore conditions, not problems, and so should be accepted.

So what is in our control? What are the kinds of things we should place into our problem basket? What are the things we should seek to change, the problems to be fixed? First and foremost, our own voluntary actions, the things we do and say, and secondly, the meditations of our hearts. By meditations I mean the thoughts and the values we deliberately bring to mind, the ones we chose to focus on, and that we use to guide our lives.

We can treat people better, we can speak kindly, we can choose to act with courage even if we feel afraid, we can act with hospitality, we can listen. We can be kind to strangers, even those who do not elicit instinctive sympathy within us. We can be authentic, not to the passing thoughts or feelings of a moment, but to our core beliefs and values, the ones we choose, meditate on and hold dear.

Viktor Frankl said, "When we are no longer able to change a situation, we are challenged to change ourselves."

He called this freedom:

> We who lived in concentration camps can remember the men who walked through the huts comforting others, giving away their last piece of bread. They may have been few in number, but they offer sufficient proof that everything can be taken from a man but one thing: the last of the human freedoms – to choose one's attitude in any given set of circumstances, to choose one's own way.

> Forces beyond your control can take away everything you possess except one thing, your freedom to choose how you will respond to the situation."

It is not freedom from conditions, but it is freedom to take a stand toward the conditions.

Significantly, the courage we need is the courage to change ourselves, to take responsibility for our actions and decisions, for more than anything else it is our voluntary actions over which we have control and which we therefore can change.

The next line reads, "living one day at a time". As Jesus said in Matthew Chapter 6 verse 34:

> Do not worry about tomorrow, for tomorrow will worry about itself. Each day has enough trouble of its own.

The human mind is like an hourglass, the experiences of our lives are processed second by second, grain by grain passing from future to past via the narrow point of now. We can usually manage life one day at a time, though sometimes when the going gets tough minute by minute is all we can bear. But if we try to rush the future forward by worrying, or refuse to let go of the past, the strongest mind will like a bunged-up hourglass break or jam. Life just won't work anymore.

The next line reads, "enjoying one moment at a time".

This is a reference to the depth of pleasure that can be found in every moment of our lives if we take notice. We can find instant joy, if we take the time to smell the flowers, see the patterns of water running down a window in the rain, hear the crunch of leaves underfoot, or notice the infinite variety of the shapes of stones that make up gravel. We can, like the innocent described in William Blake's poem, "... see a World in a Grain of Sand And a Heaven in a Wild Flower." This state of being grounded in the here and now is called mindfulness by the currently trendy but is nothing new. It is the opposite of being caught up in imagining the future or reliving the past. It is being present in the external and shared world, not absent from it like absent-minded professors going about not noticing the world.

Of course, this state of *here and now* presence is not one to seek to dwell in constantly, for the life of the mind, of human imagination is the source of our creativity and a great human treasure. What is important is to use our imaginations for good and not to inflict pain upon ourselves and others, and to be able to step into reality and see its beauty whenever we need to, so as not to become prisoners of our minds.

"Accepting hardship as a pathway to peace". The idea that hardship can be a pathway to peace may need a bit more explanation.

Viktor Frankl said the following:

> Life is never made unbearable by circumstances, but only by lack of meaning and purpose.
>
> In some ways suffering ceases to be suffering at the moment it finds a meaning, for example, the meaning of a sacrifice.

That is, when we choose to endure a hardship or unpleasant experience willingly, or deny ourselves in some way for the benefit of others, that hardship or denial can be seen as a freely offered sacrifice, and so become a path to peace and a road to happiness. Again to quote Viktor:

> Don't aim at success. The more you aim at it and make it a target, the more you are going to miss it. For success, like happiness, cannot be pursued; it must ensue, and it only does so as the unintended side effect of one's personal dedication to a cause greater than oneself.

The final section of the prayer summarises what has gone before.

"Taking, as Jesus did, This sinful world as it is, Not as I would have it," restates the need for acceptance using the life of Jesus as an example.

"Trusting that You will make all things right, If I surrender to Your will, So that I may be reasonably happy in this life, And supremely happy with You forever in the next."

While these lines reference hope in the life to come, they also restate the central theme of the prayer, which is that accepting God's will is the path to happiness in this world.

Next time we see or hear this familiar prayer, in its short or long form, why don't we stop and pause for a moment to think about what it says, and how the wisdom it contains can help each of us find the serenity those who pray it seek.

bibliography

Armstrong, K. (2011). A charter for compassion. *Religions*, (1), 21.

Dubois, P. (1909). Self-control and how to secure it (HH Boyd, Trans.). *New York, NY: Funk & Wagnalls.*

Engberg-Pedersen, T. (2004). Stoicism in the apostle Paul: a philosophical reading. *Stoicism: traditions and transformations*, 52-75.

Harris, R. (2022). *The happiness trap: How to stop struggling and start living.* Shambhala Publications.

Hayes, S. C., Strosahl, K. D., & Wilson, K. G. (1999). Acceptance and commitment therapy: an experimental approach to behavior change. Guilford. *New York.*

James, W. (1899). Talks to Teachers on Psychology, and to Students on some of Life's Ideals. Henry Holt & Co. *New York.*

Kessler, D., & Kubler-Ross, E. (2005). *On grief and grieving.* Scribner.

Kreston, R. (2014). Paved With Good Intentions: Mao Tse-Tung's Four Pests Disaster." *Discover. Science for the curious.*

MacLean, P. D. (1990). *The triune brain in evolution: Role in paleocerebral functions.* Springer Science & Business Media.

Meadows, G. (2014). *The Sleep Book: How to sleep well every night.* Hachette UK.

Schweitzer, A. (1956). *Memoirs of Childhood and Youth. Translated by CT Campion.* Allen Unwin.

Tolle, E. (1997). The Power of Now. Namaste Publishing, Inc. *Vancouver.*

Joan White spent much of her professional life in the world of health care, where she bore witness to both the resilience and fragility of the human spirit. A lifelong seeker, Joan has been deeply drawn to the rich tapestry of philosophical, evolutionary, psychological, literary and spiritual ideas that explore what it means to be human and the art of happiness. Her writing is inspired by a desire to gathering these insights into something meaningful and practical—a resource for those grappling with sadness, worry or self-doubt.

When she's not writing, Joan finds peace in her garden, joy in her craft projects, and renewal in the wilderness. She lives with her husband in Waikanae, Wellington, New Zealand, where they enjoy spending time with their three adult children and young grandson.

Email: joanwhitewriter@gmail.com